DEBBIE MUMM'S

12 DAYS of CHRISTMAS

For independent Quilt Stores,
please place your orders through Debbie Mumm, Inc.
1116 E. Westview Ct., Spokane, Washington 99218
Toll Free: (888)819-2923
FAX: (509) 466-6919
www.debbiemumm.com

For the Book Trade and selected craft stores,
please order through Landauer Books,
12251 Maffitt Rd., Cumming, Iowa 50061
Toll Free: (800) 557-2144
FAX: (515) 287-1530
Landaucor@aol.com
ISBN# 1-890621-47-1
Or, order through your favorite Book Trade
and craft store distributor.

Debbie Mumm's 12 Days of Christmas

CREATE WARMTH AND ELEGANCE

WITH GIFT, DECORATING AND QUILTING IDEAS

DEAR FRIENDS,

Welcome to my very favorite time of year ... Christmas. I'm so pleased to bring you our newest book, *Debbie Mumm's 12 Days of Christmas.* It's a festive blend of the elegance of the holidays with the warmth of country.

We've all hummed the catchy tune of that holiday song, "The Twelve Days of Christmas," but did you know that the roots for this gracious and giving time of year go back centuries? Even in medieval times, feasting, storytelling, music, and gift giving began on Christmas and filled the next twelve days. What a perfect inspiration for our book!

We kept this little bit of history in mind as we created the delightful new projects you'll find brimming from the book's pages. From great entertaining to quick quilting, gift giving, and home décor ideas, they will help you add that special holiday sparkle to your home.

A favorite part of the traditional Twelve Days of Christmas was feasting and entertaining, and we'll help make it easy for you to keep up the tradition! For the first time our book includes scrumptious menus and recipes. For even more fun, get the whole family involved. In fact, put Dad in charge of the Christmas brunch! We've done all the planning. With the help of the rest of the family, all he needs to do is the cooking.

To serve an elegant Christmas dinner, we've used my festive Twelve Days of Christmas dinnerware, which is a wonderful collector's set for your holiday entertaining. The lovely artwork seen throughout the book is also featured on the dinnerware.

And that's only the beginning. Dozens of fun and fanciful ideas are waiting for you inside *Debbie Mumm's 12 Days of Christmas.* Enjoy them all. We've enjoyed creating them for you in the rich and rewarding spirit of the holidays.

May your Twelve Days of Christmas be filled with family, friends, and the gracious giving that makes this season the most wonderful time of the year!

Merry Christmas,

Debbie Mumm

1116 E. Westview Ct., Spokane, WA 99218-1384

(509) 466-3572 • Fax (509) 466-6919 • Toll Free (888) 819-2923 • www.debbiemumm.com

TABLE OF CONTENTS

A PARTRIDGE IN A PEAR TREE

A PARTRIDGE IN A PEAR TREE

*On the first day of Christmas,
my true love sent to me,
A Partridge in a Pear Tree ...*

Wrap yourself in the true magic of the Twelve Days of Christmas. Let elegance and warmth fill your home as you celebrate with family and friends, food and song.

PARTRIDGE IN A PEAR TREE CENTERPIECE

On the first day of Christmas …
welcome the season with this elegant
centerpiece tree adorned with golden pears.
And of course, what pear tree would
be complete without its own
charming partridge!

MATERIALS NEEDED

Terra cotta or metal
   square-sided flowerpot
   approximately 6" x 6"
Plastic pears, ten to twelve
   small (2" to 2⅜" long)
All-purpose flat spray primer
Clear ruler
Soft-lead pencil
Scotch® Brand™ Magic Tape
   (do not use substitutes)
Acrylic craft paint
   antique white, gold,
   black, red, green, gray,
   dark brown

Assorted paintbrushes
Small natural sponge
Spray matte varnish
Antiquing medium
Toothbrush
Green florist's Styrofoam
   to fit inside pot
Small live or artificial tree
   approximately 16" tall
Moss
Transparent nylon fishline
   small gauge
Partridge Pincushion

PAINTING THE POT AND PEARS

For best results, be sure and allow time to dry thoroughly between each step.

1. Prime the pot and the small plastic pears with all-purpose flat spray primer.
2. Paint the body of the pot with antique white acrylic craft paint. Allow to dry. Apply two coats of gold paint to each pear.
3. Measure 1" up from the bottom of the pot and use a soft-lead pencil to draw a line all around the pot. Measure and mark a grid of ¼" squares within the 1"-wide area for the checkerboard.
4. Apply Scotch® Magic Tape™ to the pot above and along the line. Press firmly in place to protect the white paint.

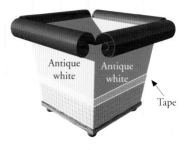

5. Paint every other square black and allow to dry. Remove the tape.

6. Apply tape along the edge of the top row of black-and-white checks. On the upper portion of the pot, draw a vertical line every ⅜". Paint every other stripe red.

7. Paint a narrow green line above the checked area and a narrow gold line at the bottom. If your pot has visible "feet," paint them green or one of the other colors you've used on the pot.

8. Paint the upper edge of the pot black. Referring to Painting Techniques on page 139, sponge black area with gray paint to give it a slightly mottled appearance. (If you have never done sponge painting, practice on scrap paper or cardboard before applying the paint to your pot.)

9. Spray the painted pot with matte-finish varnish. Following the manufacturer's directions, apply an antiquing medium.
10. When dry, spray again with matte, satin, or gloss finish.
11. Using a soft-lead pencil, sketch a design on each pear. Consider patterns of dots, checks, plaids, or stripes. Refer to page 125 for painting details. Paint designs with a contrasting color.

12. Referring to Painting Techniques on page 139, spatter paint each pear.
13. Finish each pear with a coat of spray varnish.
14. Apply antiquing medium; allow to dry. Add a final coat of spray varnish.

TIP

To make straight painted lines … after you have drawn the lines with a pencil, place tape along the marked lines in the stripes that will remain white. Press firmly in place. Use the tape edges as your painting guide.

PARTRIDGE PINCUSHION

This charming little Christmas bird makes a lovely holiday gift for any hand stitcher or quilter on your list ... or make it just for yourself!

MATERIALS NEEDED

Fabric scraps - Black, dark red, white, gold, and black/brown stripe
Thread
Lightweight batting - scraps
Polyester fiberfill - a handful
Lightweight cardboard - scraps

Feathers - brown/tan, approximately 1" x 3", for tail, (available in craft stores)
Glue stick
Glue gun and glue
Seed beads - two black for the eyes
Sand

CUTTING AND ASSEMBLY

Use the pattern pieces on pages 11-12.

1. Following the directions on pattern piece, cut the required shapes from the designated fabrics.
2. Appliqué the red, ivory, and gold face pieces to each black bird body. Satin stitch the outside curved edge of the red piece, and then add the ivory piece followed by the gold piece for the beak.

Satin Stitching

3. With right sides together, stitch the bird body pieces together along the front and top edges. End the stitching at the dot at the tail.

4. With right sides together, pin and stitch the back gusset to the bird body. Turn under and press ¼" all the way around the bottom edge of the bird.

5. Stuff the bird with a handful of polyester fiberfill, inserting a small handful of sand toward the bottom for added weight.

6. Using the seam line on the pattern for the bird base, cut a lightweight cardboard circle. Position the circle on the wrong side of the bird base and turn the fabric raw edge in. Use glue stick to hold it in place.

7. Whipstitch the base to the bottom edge of the bird. Use transparent nylon thread if you wish so the stitches don't show.

8. With right sides together and a piece of batting on bottom, stitch each pair of wing pieces together. Make a slit in the underlayer toward the top edge of the wing. Carefully turn the wing right side out through the slit.

9. Turn under ¼" and press along the straight edge of the flap for the tail. Place wrong side of flap to right side of tail. Layer the tailpieces right sides together with the batting on bottom and stitch all around. Slit the tail as you did for the wings and turn right side out.

10. Referring to the close-up photo of the partridge for positioning, use a glue gun to attach the wings and the tail.

11. Sew a black bead in place on each side of the head. Tuck the tail feathers under the flap and glue in place.

PINCUSHION TEMPLATES

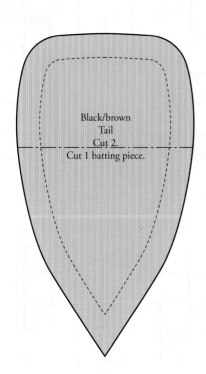

Black/brown
Tail
Cut 2.
Cut 1 batting piece.

——— · ——— Placement Guide
-------------- Stitch Line
— + — + — Fold Line

Black/brown
Flap for Tail
Cut 1.

Fold on dashed line.

TIP

ASSEMBLING THE CENTERPIECE

1. *If needed, cut florist's Styrofoam into pieces to fit and fill the interior of the pot.*

2. *If using an artificial tree, place it in the pot, inserting the stem into the foam blocks to make sure it is anchored in a stable position. Add moss around the base of the tree. If using a living tree, fill pot with planting soil and plant tree.*

3. *Cut short lengths of fine-gauge fishline and tie around pear stems. Tie the ends in an overhand knot to make a loop on each one. Arrange the pears on the tree as desired and tuck the Partridge Pincushion front and center at the base of the tree.*

AND WHAT ELSE?

They're so delightful, how about making even more partridges and painted golden pears to decorate your tree or to give as gifts? Just add a ribbon loop at the top of each partridge for hanging and they're ready for the tree.

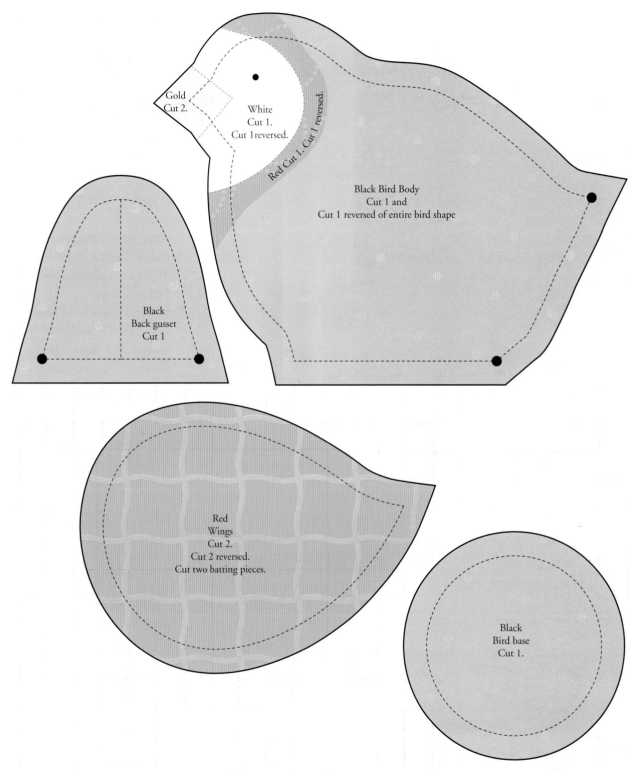

Gold
Cut 2.

White
Cut 1.
Cut 1 reversed.

Red Cut 1. Cut 1 reversed.

Black Bird Body
Cut 1 and
Cut 1 reversed of entire bird shape

Black
Back gusset
Cut 1

Red
Wings
Cut 2.
Cut 2 reversed.
Cut two batting pieces.

Black
Bird base
Cut 1.

PINCUSHION TEMPLATES

COUNTDOWN TO CHRISTMAS CALENDAR

Everyone loves a surprise …

especially at Christmas. Each day

open the door to an attic window to count

down the twelve days before Christmas.

Untie the ribbon around each pretty

button to find the day's surprise.

Finished Size: 20½" x 25"

FABRIC REQUIREMENTS

Fabric A *(window behind the door)*
   12 fussy cut 3½" motifs
   or ¼ yard

Fabric B *(tan window frame–side)*
   ⅙ yard

Fabric C *(brown windowsill
   bottom)* - ⅙ yard

Fabric D *(red print for doors)***
   ⅓ yard

Fabric E *(green print for doors)***
   ⅓ yard

** *You can use three different
   sets of red and green prints
   for the doors (as in the quilt
   shown) if you prefer.*

Accent Border *(green print)*
   ⅛ yard

Border *(red/green/tan plaid)*
   ¼ yard

Binding *(brown)* - ¼ yard

Backing - ⅞ yard

Lightweight batting
   24½" x 29" piece

Green ribbon - 4½ yards
   of ¼" - wide

Porcelain buttons - Twelve
   of Christmas theme
   *We used Christmas buttons
   from Porcelain Rose (See
   resource listing on page 139).*

FABRIC REQUIREMENTS

Fabric A - *(windows)*
  Two 3½" x 42" strips, cut into
  • Twelve 3½" squares
Fabric B *(window frame)*
  Two 2" x 42" strips, cut into
  • Twelve 2" x 5" pieces
Fabric C *(windowsill)*
  Two 2" x 42" strips, cut into
  • Twelve 2" squares
  • Twelve 2" x 3½" pieces
Fabric D *(red for doors)*
  One 3½" x 42" strip, cut into
  • Six 3½" squares
  Three 1½" x 42" strips, cut into
  • Three 1½" x 14" strips
  • Two 1½" x 3½ pieces
  • Four 1½" x 2½" pieces
  • Thirty-two 1½" squares

Fabric E *(green for doors)*
  One 3½" x 42" strip, cut into
  • Six 3½" squares
  Four 1½" x 42" strips, cut into
  • Three 1½" x 14" pieces
  • Ten 1½" x 3½" pieces
  • Four 1½" x 2½" pieces
  • Twenty 1½" squares
Accent Border
  Two 1½" x 42" strips
Border
  Two 2½" x 42" strips*
Binding
  Two 2¾" x 42" strips*
  *If the strips are not
  at least 42" long, cut a third
  border strip*

CUTTING THE STRIPS AND PIECES

Pre-wash and press fabrics. Using rotary cutter, see-through ruler, and cutting mat, cut the following strips and pieces. If indicated, some will need to be cut again into smaller strips and pieces. The approximate width of the fabric is 42". Measurements for all the pieces include ¼" seam allowance.

MAKING THE ATTIC WINDOWS

1. To make quick corner triangles, (see page 138) use a ruler to mark one diagonal line on the wrong side of each 2" Fabric C square. Place each marked square face down at one end of each 2" x 5" Fabric B piece and stitch on the line. Cut ¼" from the stitching. Press the seam allowance toward the resulting triangle.

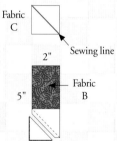

2. Sew a 2" x 3½" Fabric C piece to the bottom edge of each Fabric A 3½" square. Press the seam toward the square. Sew the window frames made in step 1 to the right-hand edge of each square. Press the seam toward the square.

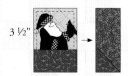

MAKING THE DOORS

You will make three different nine-patch blocks for a total of twelve doors — one for each Attic Window Block.

Ninepatch
Make 2.

Ninepatch
Make 2.

Wreath
Make 4.

Friendship Star
Make 2.

Friendship Star
Make 2.

NINE PATCH DOORS

1. Sew the 1½" x 14" strips of Fabric D and E together in units to make strip sets 1 and 2. Press the seams toward the red strips in each. Using a rotary cutter and ruler, cut six 1½" segments from strip set 1 and six 1½" segments from strip set 2

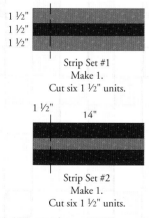

1½"
1½"
1½"

Strip Set #1
Make 1.
Cut six 1 ½" units.

1½"   14"

Strip Set #2
Make 1.
Cut six 1 ½" units.

2. Arrange the segments to create four nine patch blocks. Sew the pieces together for each block and press the seams in one direction.

Make 2.   Make 2.

FRIENDSHIP STAR DOORS

1. Use a ruler and sharp pencil to mark one diagonal line on the wrong side of eight 1½" Fabric D and eight 1½" Fabric E squares. Place a marked Fabric D square face down at each end of two 1½" x 3½" Fabric E pieces with the marked lines positioned as shown. Stitch on the line. Cut away the corners ¼" from the stitching. Press the seam allowance toward the resulting triangle. Repeat with 1½" Fabric E squares and Fabric D 1½" x 3½" pieces. You should have four squares of Fabrics D and E left for the next step.

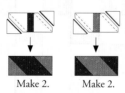

Make 2.   Make 2.

2. Place a Fabric E 1½" square face down at one end of four 1½" x 2½" Fabric D pieces and stitch on the lines. Cut away the corners ¼" from the stitching. Press the seam allowances toward the triangles. Repeat with the remaining Fabric D squares and Fabric E 1½" x 2½" pieces.

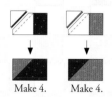

Make 4.   Make 4.

3. Arrange the pieced units with 1½" Fabric D and E squares to create four star blocks. Sew the pieces together in rows; sew the rows together and press the seams in one direction.

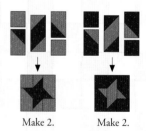

Make 2.   Make 2.

WREATH DOORS

1. Use a ruler and sharp pencil to mark one diagonal line on the wrong side of sixteen 1½" Fabric D squares. Place a marked Fabric D square face down at each end of each 1½" x 3½" Fabric E pieces, with the marked lines positioned as shown. Stitch on the lines. Cut away the corners ¼" from the stitching. Press the seam allowances toward the resulting triangles.

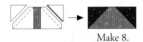

Make 8.

2. Sew a Fabric E 1½" square to opposite sides of four Fabric D 1½" squares. Press the seams toward the red squares.

3. Arrange the pieced units to create four wreath blocks. Sew the rows together for each block and press the seams in one direction.

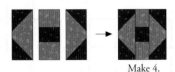

Make 4.

4. Making angled cuts, cut twelve pieces of ¼"-wide ribbon, each 14½" long. Fold each piece in half and pin one to the center point of one edge of each nine-patch block. Pin or baste in place.

5. With right sides together, sew each completed nine-patch block to a 3½" square of Fabric D or E, leaving one edge unstitched. Turn right side out and press.

ASSEMBLY

1. Referring to the quilt layout, arrange the completed Attic Window Blocks in four rows of three blocks each. Sew together in vertical rows of four blocks each. Press seams of adjoining rows in opposite directions.

2. Pin a door to each attic window block making sure to position so the window is completely hidden. Stitch in place.

3. Join the rows and press seams in one direction.

ADDING THE BORDERS

1. From each accent border strip, cut two 1½" x 14" pieces and two 1½" x 20½" pieces. Sew the shorter strips to the top and bottom edges of the quilt. Sew the longer strips to the sides.

2. From each of the two plaid border strips, cut two 2½" x 16" pieces and two 2½" x 24½" pieces. Sew the shorter strips to the top and bottom edges of the quilt. Sew the longer strips to the sides.

Note: If you cut three border strips because the fabric was less than 42" wide, sew the strips together, end to end, press the seams open, and cut the required border lengths from the continuous strip.

LAYERING AND FINISHING

1. Cut a 24½" x 29" piece of backing fabric. Arrange and baste the backing, batting, and quilt top together, referring to Layering the Quilt directions on page 138.

2. Machine or hand quilt.

3. Referring to Binding the Quilt directions on page 139, attach the shorter binding strips to the top and bottom edges and the longer binding strips to the sides of the quilt.

4. Sew a button to the window frame to the right of each patchwork door. Tie each ribbon in a bow around its button.

CREATE THE SURPRISE!

Use your imagination to create the Christmas surprise behind each door. Use a fabric with fanciful holiday motifs and cut a design to fit in each window. Or how about buttons? Charming porcelain buttons with animal themes will be a hit with children. For the antique lover, stitch a vintage button behind each door. What fun to open a different door each day to see what surprise it holds!

TWO TURTLE DOVES

TWO TURTLE DOVES

On the second day of Christmas,
my true love sent to me,
Two Turtledoves…

Share in the loving spirit of these two little turtledoves by creating a holiday season brimming over with graciousness and giving.

WELCOME HOME BANNER

Two little turtledoves bill and coo
above their happy home in this
delightful birdhouse banner.
Hang it inside or on your front
door for a festive welcome
to holiday guests.

Finished Size: 16⅝" x 27¾"

FABRIC REQUIREMENTS

Fabric A (*dark green for roof*)
⅛ yard
Fabric B (*gold for roof accent*)
⅛ yard
Fabric C (*birdhouse*) - ⅝ yard
Fabric D (*black for checkerboard*)
⅛ yard
Fabric E (*light tan for*
checkerboard) - ⅛ yard
Fabric F (*rust-red for base and*
backing) - 1 yard
Fabric G (*dark green for wreath*)
7" x 14" piece
Fabric H (*three dark greens*)
⅛ yard each
Fabric I (*black birdhouse door*)
One 3" square

Fabric J (*assorted tan, gold,*
and brown prints for doves)
Scraps of eight dark
and light prints
Lightweight fusible web - ¼ yard
Wire-edged ribbon (*red*)
½ yard of 1½"- wide
Beads five or six red for berries
Embroidery floss or perle
cotton, gold, black, and
brown
Satin ribbon (*burgundy*)
½ yard of ⅛"- wide
Lightweight batting - 1 yard
Ribbon (*green*) - ¼ yard of
¼"- wide
Cord or ribbon (*gold*)
¼ yard of narrow cord

CUTTING THE STRIPS AND PIECES

Read first paragraph of Cutting
the Strips and Pieces on page 14.
Fabric A (*roof*)
One 1½" x 42" strip, cut into
• One 1½" x 19½" strip
• One 1½" x 17½" strip
Fabric B (*accent roof*)
One 1" x 42" strip, cut into
• One 1" x 16" strip
• One 1" x 15" strip

Fabric C (*upper birdhouse*)
    One 11½" x 18" piece
Fabric D (*checkerboard*)
    Two 1½" x 42" strips, cut into
    • Three 1½" x 18" strips
Fabric E (*checkerboard*)
    Two 1½" x 42" strips, cut into
    • Three 1½" x 18" strips
Fabric F (*base and backing*)
    One 21" x 32" piece
    One 2" x 14½" strip
Fabric G (*wreath*) - Two 7" squares
Fabric H (*leaves*) - One 4" x 16"
    strip of each of three green
    fabrics
Fabric J (*birds*) - See directions
    for Making the Doves.
Batting
    One 21" x 32" piece
    One 7" x 7" piece
    Two 5" x 8" pieces

MAKING THE BANNER

1. Using a ruler and soft-lead
   pencil, draw cutting lines for
   roof on wrong side of Fabric C
   11½" x 18" piece. Cut on
   drawn lines. Trace 2" circle on
   fusiable web. Apply fusible
   web to wrong side of Fabric I
   for "door." Cut out circle and
   fuse in place on upper
   birdhouse. Machine satin
   stitch over raw edges of circle.

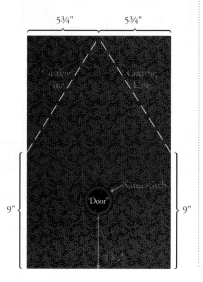

2. Trace lettering for Welcome
   on page 23 and outline stitch
   on birdhouse (refer to photo
   for placement), using black
   perle cotton or three strands
   of embroidery floss.

3. Sew shorter accent roof strip
   to left side of roof. Use rotary
   ruler and cutter to trim upper
   end of strip even with right
   edge of birdhouse. Add longer
   accent strip to remaining side.
   Trim. Repeat with dark roof
   strips. Cut lower ends of roof
   at a 45° angle. Press.

4. To make checkerboard, sew
   Fabric D and E 1½" x 18"
   strips together, alternating
   colors. Press seams toward
   darker strips. Using a rotary
   ruler and cutter, cut into
   eleven 1½"-wide segments.

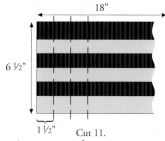

5. Arrange and sew strips in a
   checkerboard pattern,
   matching seam intersections.
   Press seams in one direction.
   Sew Fabric F 2" x 14½" piece
   to bottom edge of
   checkerboard, center it so
   same amount extends beyond
   each short edge of checkerboard. Sew checkerboard to
   bottom edge of upper
   birdhouse. Press seams away
   from checkerboard.

MAKING THE WREATH

1. Draw a 6½"-diameter circle
   on wrong side of one 7"
   square of Fabric G. Draw a
   2¼"-diameter circle in center.

2. With right sides together and
   the circle tracing on top, place
   7" squares of Fabric G on
   top of 7" batting square. Pin.
   Stitch on 6½"drawn circle and
   cut out circle, leaving a scant
   ³⁄₁₆" seam allowance all
   around. Cut out center circle
   through all layers and turn
   wreath right side out. Stitch
   ¼" from inner circle edge. Pink
   the edges.

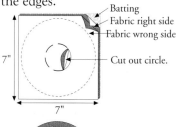

3. Apply a 4" x 8" strip of fusible
   web to half of each 4" x 16"
   strip of green fabric for leaves.
   Remove paper backing, fold
   each strip in half and fuse
   the layers together, following
   manufacturer's directions.

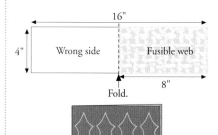

Trace 4 on each green strip.

4. Trace holly leaf template on
   page 23. Trace four leaf

shapes on each piece of doubled and fused green fabric. Cut out. Machine stitch a vein pattern on each leaf.

5. Arrange leaves on wreath and hand or machine tack in place. Tie red ribbon into a bow and tack to bottom of wreath; cut ribbon ends at an angle to prevent raveling. Sew beads to wreath in desired locations.

MAKING THE DOVES

1. Using dove pattern pieces, trace head, body, and tail shapes onto desired fabrics, making sure to trace one reversed of each shape. Cut out on traced lines.

2. With right sides together, sew a head and tail to each body. Press seams toward head and tail. Sew ribbon trim in place over seam lines on one right and one left-facing dove.

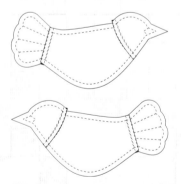

3. Place each ribbon-trimmed dove right side up on top of a 5" x 8" piece of batting. Place remaining doves face down on their mates with raw edges even. Pin in place. Stitch ¼" from raw edges through all layers. Trim. Make a small slit in top layer only of each bird.

Turn right side out through slit. Press lightly. Whipstitch slit edges together.

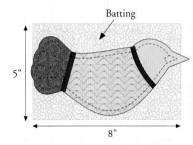

4. Using pattern pieces, trace large and small wings onto desired fabrics, leaving at least ¼" of fabric around each shape. Place fabric with drawn shapes right sides together with matching fabric piece and a layer of batting on bottom. Stitch on drawn lines. Cut out a scant 3/16" from stitching. Make a small slit in the underside only of each wing piece (as you did for the doves), taking care to make cut in the correct layer so you have a left and right of each wing size. Turn right side out through slit. Whipstitch slit edges together.

5. Embellish wings and birds with embroidery, following directions on pattern pieces.

6. Referring to finished bird photo on page 19 for positioning, tack wings to body.

LAYERING AND FINISHING

1. Place 21" x 32" batting piece on a flat surface. Place 21" x 32" backing on top with right side up. With right sides together, pin and stitch birdhouse to batting/backing layers, leaving a 4" opening

along bottom edge for turning. Pivot carefully at all corners. Trim batting and backing layers even with banner edges. Clip inward corners to, but not through, stitching. Trim corners and points to eliminate bulk.

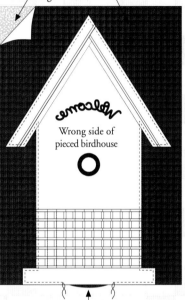

2. Turn right side out and press, turn under opening at bottom edge and slipstitch.

3. Machine or hand quilt.

4. Position wreath on banner around birdhouse "door" and hand stitch in place.

5. Referring to photo on page 19, position doves at roofline, loop the gold cord and green ribbon from beak to beak, and tack in place.

6. On back make a small thread loop for hanging. Use doubled thread and take several long, loose stitches, then cover the loop with condensed buttonhole stitches.

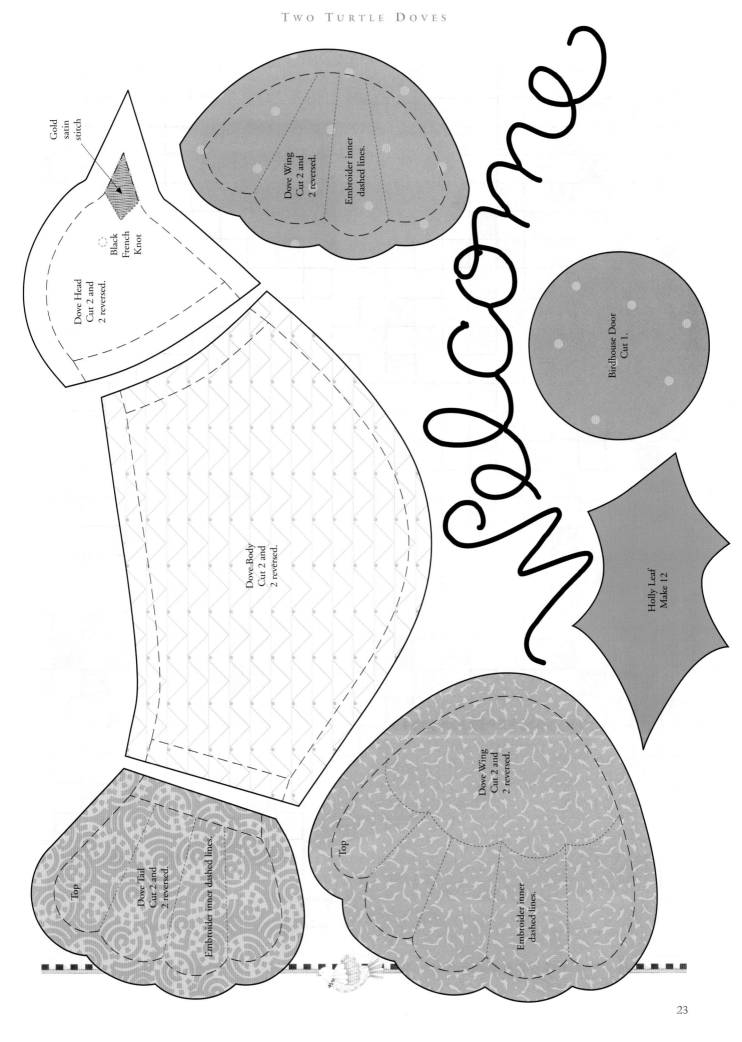

Gold satin stitch

Dove Head
Cut 2 and
2 reversed.

Black French Knot

Dove Wing
Cut 2 and
2 reversed.
Embroider inner dashed lines.

Birdhouse Door
Cut 1.

Dove Body
Cut 2 and
2 reversed.

Holly Leaf
Make 12

Welcome

Top

Dove Tail
Cut 2 and
2 reversed.
Embroider inner dashed lines.

Top

Dove Wing
Cut 2 and
2 reversed.
Embroider inner dashed lines.

BIRD FEEDER

Share your holiday spirit with the neighborhood birds too. All it takes is a little paint to transform a purchased bird feeder into an inviting spot for them to feast while you enjoy your holiday dinner inside.

MATERIALS NEEDED

Wooden birdfeeder - Unfinished, approximately (9" x 18")
Acrylic craft paints - red, ivory, black, gold, dark green, medium green
Clear ruler
Soft-lead pencil
Assorted paintbrushes
Crackle medium
Spray matte varnish
Antiquing medium
Toothbrush
Marine varnish (from hardware store)

Unfinished Feeder

PAINTING THE FEEDER

For best results, allow to dry thoroughly between steps.

1. Paint sides of feeder red. Paint front perch area ivory.
2. Using a clear ruler and soft-lead pencil, draw a ⅜" grid for checkerboard. Paint every other square black.
3. Add gold accent borders to edge of roof and edge of checkerboard.
4. Paint perches dark green and roof black.
5. Following manufacturer's directions, apply crackle medium to roof. Allow to dry thoroughly and follow with a top-coat of medium green paint.
6. Spray feeder with a coat of matte varnish. Apply antiquing medium following manufacturer's directions.
7. Referring to Painting Techniques on page 139, spatter roof with black paint.
8. To make feeder durable for outside use, apply two to three coats of marine varnish. This will tend to yellow the finished project, adding to its antiqued appearance.

WREATH PILLOW

On your favorite cozy chair by the fire, or in the guest bedroom to welcome holiday visitors, this charming appliquéd pillow will add a festive touch of the season wherever you put it.

Finished Size: 16" diameter

FABRIC REQUIREMENTS

Fabric A (*three different greens*) ¼ yard each

Fabric B (*dark green for pillow top and backing*) ½ yard

Fabric C (*gold pillow center*) 6" square

Fabric D (*red bow*) - ¼ yard

Backing - ½ yard

Thin batting - 1 yard

Pillow form - 16"-diameter

Buttons - fourteen assorted red, and gold (⅞" to 1"-diameter)

CUTTING THE STRIPS AND PIECES

Read first paragraph of Cutting the Strips and Pieces on page 14.

Fabric A - *See Making the Leaves at right.*

Fabric B -
One 16½"-diameter circle
Two 11" x 16½" pieces

Fabric C - One 4⅞"-diameter circle (*use template on page 27*)

Fabric D - One 7½" x 42" strip

Backing - One 18" x 18" square

Batting - One 18" x 18" square
Three 9" x 20" strips
One 3½" x 42" strip

MAKING THE LEAVES

1. Fold each leaf Fabric A in half crosswise with right sides together. Trace leaf templates on page 27 on wrong side of each Fabric A, leaving at least ½" of space between leaves. Trace a total of ten small and twelve large leaves.

2. With leaf tracings face up, place each folded fabric strip on top of a matching strip of batting. Stitch on lines for each leaf shape, stitching through all layers.

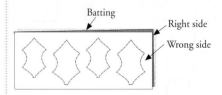

3. Cut out leaves a scant ³⁄₁₆" from the stitching. Clip curves. Make a small slit in one fabric layer of each leaf and turn right side out through slit. Press.

4. Using contrasting thread, stitch a vein pattern on each leaf.

Make 10 small,
12 large.

MAKING THE QUILTED PILLOW TOP

1. Referring to Hand Appliqué instructions on page 138, appliqué Fabric C center to center of pillow-top circle.

2. Layer backing and batting with pillow top and machine quilt in a meandering pattern on wreath and center circle. Trim batting and backing even with pillow-top edge.

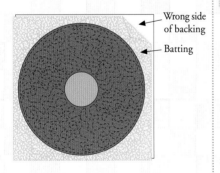

Wrong side
of backing

Batting

3. Referring to photo, arrange leaves on pillow top as desired. Tack in place with a few stitches underneath each one, leaving leaf edges free. Sew buttons in place in desired arrangement.

ASSEMBLING THE PILLOW

1. On one long edge of each 11" x 16½" Fabric B piece, turn under ¼"; turn again and machine stitch in place. Lap hemmed edges 4½" and baste together.

2. Trim to a 16½" circle for pillow backing.

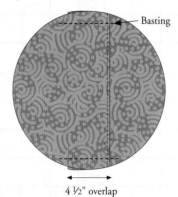

Basting

4 ½" overlap

3. With right sides together and taking care to tuck leaves out of the way of the seam allowance, stitch pillow top to pillow backing.

4. Turn pillow cover right side out.

5. To make bow, fold Fabric D strip in half lengthwise and stitch ¼" from long edges, leaving a 2"-long opening at center for turning. Press seam open or to one side. Fold strip so seam is centered.

6. With strip still wrong side out, tie into a temporary bow and position on pillow top to determine desired length. Trim short ends as needed, allowing for ¼"-wide seam allowances at each end. Untie bow and press to remove wrinkles.

7. Trim 3½"-wide batting strip to match length of bow strip. Place batting strip on unseamed side of bow strip. Stitch ¼" from each short end. Turn right side out with batting strip inside. Press lightly. Slipstitch opening closed.

Batting strip on bottom

Slipstitch opening.

8. Tie finished strip into bow and tack to the pillow top in the desired location, taking care not to catch the pillow backing in the stitches.

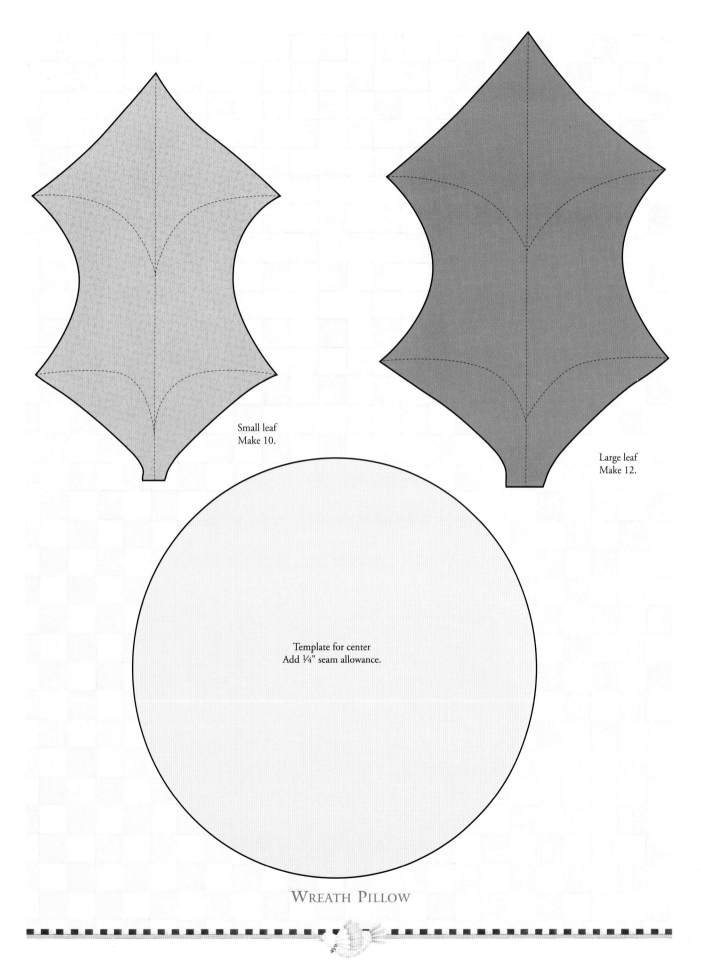

Small leaf
Make 10.

Large leaf
Make 12.

Template for center
Add ¼" seam allowance.

WREATH PILLOW

THREE FRENCH HENS

THREE FRENCH HENS

On the third day of Christmas,
my true love sent to me,
Three French Hens ...

Celebrate this joyous season in the French tradition of food, wine, and song. Make each of the Twelve Days of Christmas a festive occasion to remember all the year through.

FRENCH HEN TEA COZY

Keep your Christmas teapot cozy under the wings of this sweet mother hen. Even when the tea's not brewing, tuck the pot underneath and set the little hen in a special spot in the kitchen to oversee your holiday baking.

Finished Size: 10" x 13"

FABRIC REQUIREMENTS

Fabric A *(hen lower body)* ⅓ yard
Fabric B *(hen upper body)* ¼ yard
Fabric C *(wing)* - 7" x 30" strip
Fabric D *(face)* - 5" x 10" piece
Felted wool - scraps of gold, red, and dark brown
Black beads - Two for eyes
Lining - ⅓ yard

Lightweight batting
Two 10" x 13" pieces for hen
One 10" x 10" piece for gussets
One 7" x 15" piece for wings
Fusible web *(for Quick Fuse Appliqué only)*

CUTTING THE PIECES

Cut the pieces for hen from desired fabrics (see photo at left), following cutting directions on pattern pieces on pages 32-35.

Before you cut, decide whether you will hand appliqué the accents or use Quick-Fuse Appliqué method on pages 138 and 139. Be sure to cut one of each fabric piece reversed.

MAKING THE HEN

1. Sew outer edges of the tail, comb, beak, and wattle together with a short, closely spaced blanket stitch, referring to Embroidery Stitch Guide on page 138. Set aside.

2. Hand appliqué upper body and face to each hen body—or use the Quick-Fuse Appliqué method. Add face in same manner.

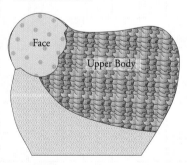

3. Place each hen on top of a 10" x 13" batting piece. Pin in place and machine or hand quilt as desired. Place front and back gussets on 10" x 10" batting piece and quilt in same manner. Trim batting even with edges of hen.

4. With right sides together and batting on bottom, stitch wings together ¼" from raw edges. Make a slit in top layer of each wing and turn wings right side out.

5. Position tail, comb, beak, and wattle in position on one hen and baste in place.

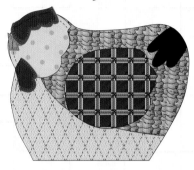

6. Position wings with slit side against hen and machine stitch in place.

7. Stitch hens right sides together, beginning and ending at dots (ends of tail and wattle). Backstitch at beginning and end of stitching. Repeat with the lining, leaving a 4"-long opening at top edge for turning.

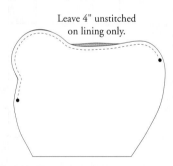

Leave 4" unstitched on lining only.

8. With right sides together, stitch gussets to hen, watching dots and edges. Repeat for lining.

9. Tuck hen inside lining with right sides together and raw edges even. Stitch lining to bottom edge of hen. Turn right side out through opening in lining top edge.

Opening in lining

Wrong side of hen

10. Turn under and press lining edges. Edge stitch layers together.

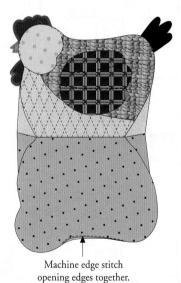

Machine edge stitch opening edges together.

11. Tuck lining up into hen head and sew a bead in eye position on each side, catching lining in the stitches to hold it in place. Stitch ¼" from bottom of hen, making sure lining doesn't peek out at lower edge.

French Hen Cozy Templates

Tail
Felted wool
Cut 2.

Front gusset
Cut one and cut one from lining.

Back gusset
Cut one.
Cut one from lining.

FRENCH HEN COZY TEMPLATE
Enlarge template to 150% – this page only.

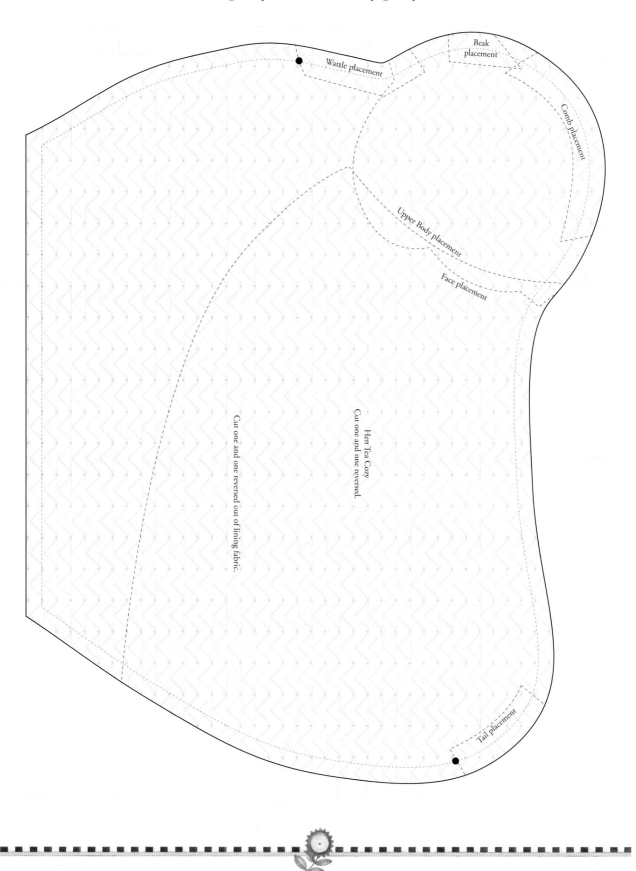

Beak placement

Wattle placement

Comb placement

Upper Body placement

Face placement

Hen Tea Cozy
Cut one and one reversed.

Cut one and one reversed out of lining fabric.

Tail placement

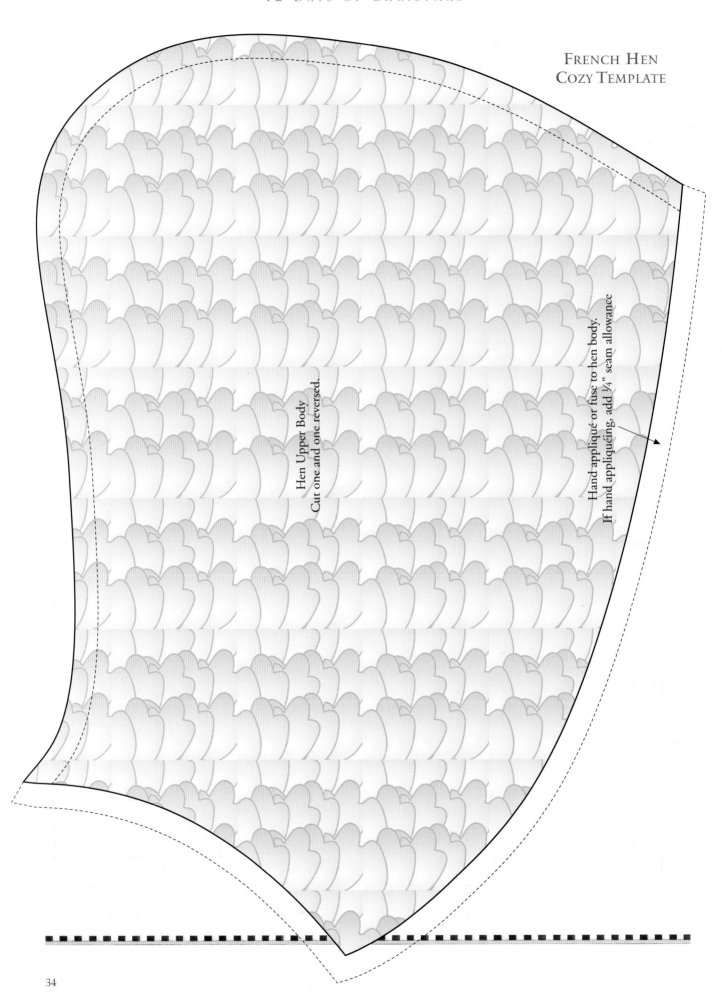

FRENCH HEN
COZY TEMPLATE

Hen Upper Body
Cut one and one reversed.

Hand appliqué or fuse to hen body.
If hand appliquéing, add ¼" seam allowance

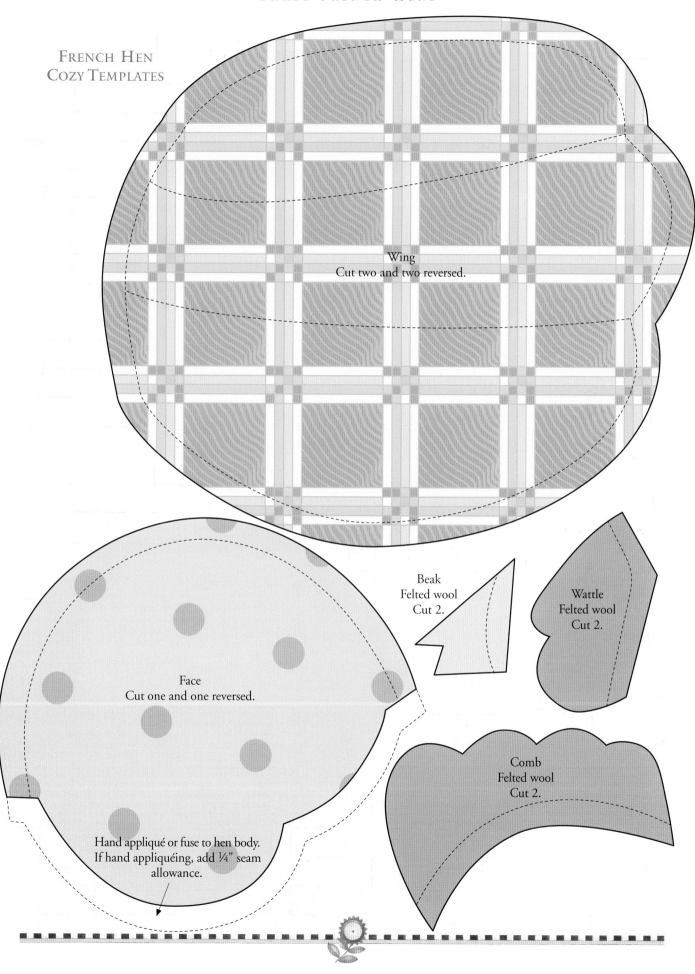

FRENCH HEN
COZY TEMPLATES

Wing
Cut two and two reversed.

Beak
Felted wool
Cut 2.

Wattle
Felted wool
Cut 2.

Face
Cut one and one reversed.

Comb
Felted wool
Cut 2.

Hand appliqué or fuse to hen body.
If hand appliquéing, add ¼" seam
allowance.

FLYING GEESE PLACEMATS

Even your casual holiday meals will be more festive when you set the table with these charming yet simple-to-sew placemats. They go together so quickly you'll want to make a set for yourself and another as a gift for a friend.

Finished size: 13" x 20"

FABRIC REQUIREMENTS

(for four placemats)

Fabric A *(center and border)*
  1 yard
Fabric B *(sashing)* - ¼ yard
Fabric C *(large triangles)*
  ½ yard

Fabric D *(small triangles)*
  ½ yard
Backing - 1½ yards
Lightweight batting or flannel
  Four 16" x 24" pieces

CUTTING THE STRIPS AND PIECES

Read first paragraph of Cutting the Strips and Pieces on page 14.

Fabric A
  Four 1" x 42" strips, cut into
  • Eight 1" x 20½" strips
  Two 11½" x 42" strips, cut into
  • Four 11½" squares
Fabric B
  Six 1" x 42" strips, cut into
  • Eight 1" x 11½" strips
  • Eight 1" x 12½" strips
Fabric C
  Six 2½" x 42" strips, cut into
  • Forty-eight 2½" x 4½" pieces
Fabric D
  Six 2½" x 42" strips, cut into
  • Ninety-six 2½" squares
Backing - Four 16" x 24" pieces

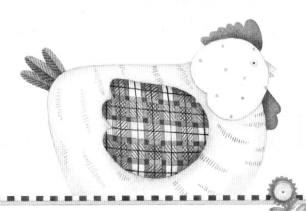

MAKING THE PLACEMATS

1. Sew a 1" x 11½" Fabric B strip to top and bottom edges of Fabric A 11½" square. Press. Sew 1" x 12½" Fabric B strips to sides. Press.

2. Make forty-eight flying geese units, using 2½" x 4½" Fabric C pieces and 2½" Fabric D squares and referring to Quick Corner Triangle directions on page 138. Press seams toward smaller triangles.

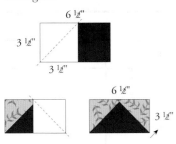

Make 48.

3. Arrange flying geese in rows of six units each. Sew units together in rows and press seam toward bottom edge of strip.

4. Sew a flying geese strip to sides of each placemat. Sew a 1" x 20½" Fabric A strip to top and bottom edges of each placemat.

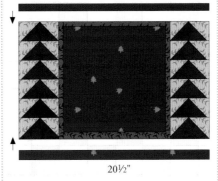

20½"

LAYERING AND FINISHING

1. Place the backing face up on top of the batting (or flannel). Center the placemat, right sides together on the backing. Stitch ¼" from placemat edges, leaving a 3" opening on one long edge for turning.

2. Trim batting and backing even with placemat edges. Turn right side out through opening. Turn in and press opening edges and slipstitch together.

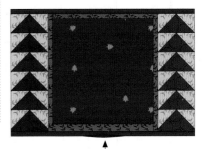

Slipstitch opening.

3. Machine or hand quilt as desired.

FRENCH HEN ADDRESS BOOK

*What an extra special gift …
a dainty-sized address book with this
charming cross-stitched French hen and your
friend's name embroidered on the cover.
Or make it for yourself to record the
names of those who will receive your
annual Christmas greeting.*

*Finished Size: Stitched area is
approximately 3½" x 3"*

CROSS STITCH SUPPLIES

Aida cloth* - 18-count antique
white, 8" x 8¼" piece
Embroidery floss - DMC
One skein of each color
(*See color legend on pg. 41*)
Tapestry needle - Size 26

**Substitute 14-count Aida cloth
for a larger image and stitching
that's easier to see (stitched area
is approximately 4½" x 3¾").*

MATERIALS NEEDED

**Completed French Hen
cross-stitch piece**
**Ring-binder-style address
book**, 9⅛" x 15½" (*open*)
Fabric A (*gold background*)
⅛ yard
Fabric B (*banner*) - 2" x 6" scrap
Fabric C (*dark red*) - ⅜ yard

Ribbon or trim (*green*) - ⅝ yard
of ½"-wide
**Black (310) DMC embroidery
floss**
Dark green cording
Cording trim (*outside edge*)
1½ yards of narrow

CROSS-STITCH DIRECTIONS

1. Following the stitch chart
and color key on page 41,
center and stitch the design
on the Aida cloth of your
choice. Refer to Embroidery
Stitch Guide on page 138.

2. Using two strands of embroidery floss for cross-stitches,
begin stitching in center of
cloth. Complete all cross-
stitching and ¼" stitches.

3. Using one strand of appropriate color floss and following the list on page 39, add
backstitched details.

Legs, polka dots, and back
(*checkerboard*) - Black (310)

Head and body - Dark Tan
(801)

Tail, wing, crown, wattle,
and eye outline - Dark
Brown (3031)

Beak - Medium Tan (434)

Lattice grid background
Two strands Gold (5282)

4. Make a French knot on "**X**"
   inside eye outline, using
   Dark Brown (3031) floss.

5. Hand wash completed
   cross-stitch piece, allow to
   dry, and press.

CUTTING THE PIECES

Fabric A (*sashing*)

One 1¼" x 42" strip
- Three 1¼" x 5" pieces
- Two 1¼" x 9⅞" pieces

Fabric B (*banner*) See step 5.

Fabric C (*book cover, lining,
and flaps*)

One 9⅞" x 42" strip, cut into
- One 9⅞" x 16¼" piece
  for lining
- One 9¾" x 9⅞" piece for
  book cover
- One 1" x 9⅞" piece for
  sashing
- Two 6½" x 9⅞" pieces
  for flaps
- One 3⅜" x 5" for book
  cover

ASSEMBLING THE COVER

1. Trim completed cross-stitch to
   4½" x 5", making sure to keep
   hen centered in piece.

2. Sew 1¼" x 5" Fabric A piece
   to top and bottom edges of
   cross-stitch piece and to
   bottom edge of 3⅜" x 5"
   Fabric C piece. Press seams
   toward strips.

3. Sew Fabric A 1¼" x 9⅞" strips
   to sides. Press seams toward
   strips. Add 1" x 9⅞" Fabric C
   strip to right-hand edge. Press
   seam toward Fabric C.

4. Sew ribbon or trim in place
   over seam lines around cross-
   stitch. Begin at one corner,
   folding mitered corners as you

go and turning under raw end
at an angle at the first corner.

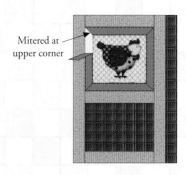

Mitered at upper corner

5. Cut appliqué banner on page
   40 from Fabric B scrap,
   adding ¼" all around for hand
   appliqué. Appliqué to book
   cover and embroider desired
   name in black. Stitch dark
   green cording to inside lines.
   Outline stitch around finished
   banner with three strands of
   black embroidery floss.

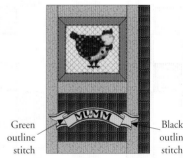

Green outline stitch

Black outline stitch

39

6. Sew pieced book front to one long edge of 9¾" x 9⅞" Fabric C piece. Press seam toward Fabric C.

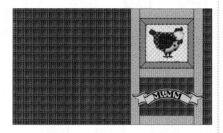

7. Fold 6½" x 9⅞" Fabric C flaps in half lengthwise with wrong sides together and position on right side of front cover. Pin or baste in place.

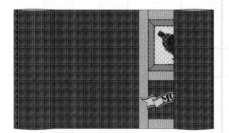

Baste flaps to lining.

8. Place 9⅞" x 16¼" Fabric C Lining piece face down on right side of cover/flap piece. Stitch around all four sides, leaving a 3" opening at short flap end. Clip corners. Turn right side out through opening. (Opening will be hidden inside flap so it doesn't require stitching.)

3" opening

9. Invisibly hand sew decorative cording to outer edges of book cover using invisible stitches and overlapping ends at an inconspicuous spot on back of cover. Treat cut ends with a seam sealant or permanent fabric glue to prevent raveling.

10. Tuck address book into flaps and fill with the names of your special friends and family.

SOMETHING EXTRA

Wallhanging   Coaster or Ornament with loop

If you love to cross-stitch, you'll want to create more holiday touches using our charming little French Hen. It will be delightful stitched to make coasters, ornaments, or wall hangings. Just add a layer of batting and backing and piping trim at outside edge for coasters and wall hanging. Add a cording hanger for wall hanging or a loop for ornaments. Mat and frame your little hen and display it on a small gold easel on an end table or bookcase.

BOOK TEMPLATE

FOUR CALLING BIRDS

FOUR CALLING BIRDS

On the fourth day of Christmas,
my true love sent to me,
Four Calling Birds ...

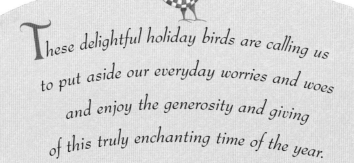

These delightful holiday birds are calling us
to put aside our everyday worries and woes
and enjoy the generosity and giving
of this truly enchanting time of the year.

CALLING BIRD CARDS

Pretty enough to frame and keep for years, these cards will certainly please the friends and family who receive them. Decorative papers, bits of fabric and trim, and you can create elegant greetings with that handmade touch.

MATERIALS NEEDED

Fabric scraps in assorted colors and designs

Lightweight fusible web

Fine-tip marking pen

Double-sided foam tape

Card stock 4½" x 6" in assorted colors and textures

Purchased blank cards 4½" x 6"

Decorative papers - including printed, textured, corrugated, flocked, and metallic papers from art or rubber stamp stores

Scissors - small, sharp

Glue stick

Double-sided tape

Scissors with decorative blades

Stamp with Christmas message

Embossing ink

Embossing powder

Heat gun or blow dryer

Envelopes - 4¾" x 6½"

Optional Embellishments:

Small glass beads

Embossable tape with embossing powder

Scented embossing powder

Assorted narrow trims

ASSEMBLING THE CARDS

1. Select purchased cards or use a rotary cutter and ruler to cut cardstock into 6" x 9" pieces. Fold in half crosswise and make a sharp crease.
2. Referring to photograph at left for design ideas, cut and layer the decorative papers in desired shapes and sizes, using two or three for each card to add depth. Decorate outside edges of paper pieces if desired with beads, embossing (see embossing directions at right), or narrow trims.
3. Center and glue paper layers in place in desired order on card front.
4. Prepare bird bodies following directions for Quick-Fuse Appliqué, on page 139. Cut out all shapes on drawn lines and fuse bodies and upper wings only to cardstock.
5. Position lower wing on bird body and fuse in place.
6. Cut a small piece of foam tape and use to adhere upper wing to bird, lifting it from the surface for added dimension. Position top layer of ribbon (piece 6) on goose's neck in same manner. Fuse beaks in place and add beak details with fine-point pen.
7. Position bird on card and glue in place.
8. Make a banner using Christmas stamp, embossable inks, and embossing powders. Position on cards and glue in place.

EMBOSSING DIRECTIONS

1. Use embossing ink on the stamp and then stamp image on desired paper.
2. Cover stamped image with generous amount of embossing powder.
3. After covering entire stamped image, pour excess powder back into jar. Tap paper gently to remove the loose powder as you pour it into jar.
4. Using a heat gun or a blow dryer at lowest speed, heat back side of image. The powder will melt and change color when ready.

CARD TEMPLATES

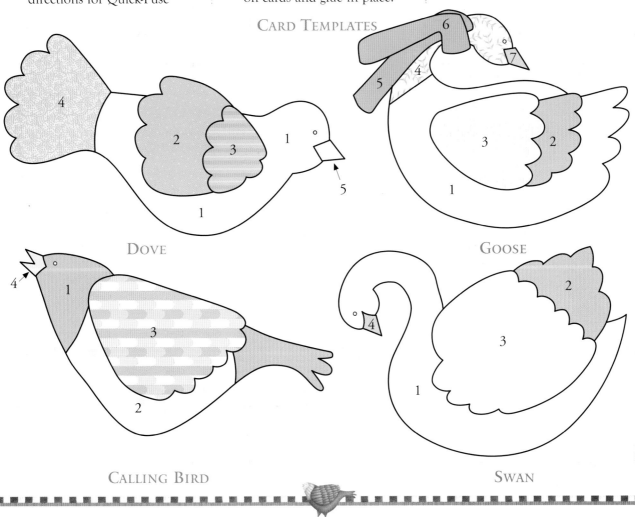

DOVE

GOOSE

CALLING BIRD

SWAN

EMBOSSED VELVET BASKET LINER

Calling on friends during the holiday adds to the fun and shares the spirit of the season. When you make your Christmas calls, deliver special treats in a basket lined with this elegant embossed velvet square.

MATERIALS NEEDED

Fabric A - Velvet - ⅔ yard rayon/acetate* (*makes two liners*)

Fabric B - Lining fabric - ⅔ yard matching or contrasting

Tassels - Four matching or contrasting colors (2½" or 3" long) for each liner

Rubber stamp in design of your choice

Water in mister bottle

Iron and ironing board

Avoid nylon velvet, as it is difficult to make deep, lasting impressions in this resilient fiber.

CUTTING THE PIECES

Fabric A - Two 22" squares
Fabric B - Two 18½" squares

EMBOSSING THE VELVET

1. Preheat iron to a dry setting between wool and cotton (*medium-hot*).
2. Position velvet square face down on the rubber stamp in desired position. Mist lightly with water.
3. Press with iron for 20 to 30 seconds and lift iron straight up from fabric. Do not slide! You will see design on the wrong side; peel velvet away from stamp to see embossing on right side.

Design shows on wrong side when you lift iron.

4. Reposition fabric in next desired location and stamp again. Repeat until you have embossed entire piece as desired, extending designs all the way out to velvet raw edges.

MAKING THE LINER

1. Using a rotary cutter and ruler, trim embossed velvet piece to 18½" square.
2. Machine baste a tassel to right side of each corner of velvet square, stitching several times to attach securely.

3. With tassels inside, right sides together, and raw edges even, sew lining square to velvet square ¼" from raw edges. Begin just past center of one edge and backstitch. Leave a 3"-long opening for turning and backstitch. Clip corners, cutting away excess tassel loop.
4. Turn right side out and finger press edges carefully from lining side to avoid flattening embossing. Turn in raw edges of opening and slipstitch closed.
5. Drape velvet square over basket edges and fill with gifts and goodies to take to special friends on your gift list.

FIVE GOLDEN RINGS

FIVE GOLDEN RINGS

*On the fifth day of Christmas,
my true love sent to me,
Five Golden Rings ...*

Nothing says elegance like touches of glittering gold. Your Christmas dinner table will take on an aura of holiday magic when you add that special sparkle of gold.

HAND BELL CHOIR

"Ring" in the holidays with this elegant mantle-cover edged with enchanting beaded trim. Add the glow of candles in brass holders, and just imagine the ringing of the bells on Christmas morning!

Finished Size: 19" x 45"

FABRIC REQUIREMENTS

Fabric A (*bells*)
  One 6½" x 10" piece of each of five different fabrics
Fabric B (*black background, sashing and top of cover*) - 1 yard
Decorative ribbons and trims
  6" lengths of assorted 2½" to 3"-wide
Decorative trim - 6" lengths of narrow (*optional*)

Backing - 1 yard
Batting - 23" x 49" piece
Buttons
  Five ⅝"-diameter assorted gold
  Five 1"-diameter assorted gold
Beaded fringe -1½ yards

CUTTING THE STRIPS AND PIECES

Read first paragraph of Cutting the Strips and Pieces on page 14.

Fabric A - For each block, cut
  One 5½" x 6½" piece
  One 1⅞" circle
  One 1½" x 2½" piece
  Two 1½" squares

Fabric B - *(for all five blocks, sashing, and mantel top)*
  Five 2½" x 42" strips, cut into
  • One 2½" x 40" piece
  • One 2½" x 10" piece
  • Ten 2½" x 4½" pieces
  • Ten 2½" x 6½" pieces
  One 1½" x 42" strip, cut into
  • Ten 1½" squares
  Two 3½" x 42" strips, cut into
  • Five 3½" x 9½" pieces
  Two 6½" x 42" strips
  • One 6½" x 40" piece
  • One 6½" x 10" piece

Backing - One 23 x 42" strip
  One 7½" x 23" strip

MAKING THE BELLS

1. For each bell center, sew a 1½" square of Fabric B to each upper corner of each 5½" x 6½" piece of Fabric A. Follow directions for Quick Corner Triangles on page 138. Press seams toward triangles.

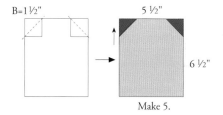

Make 5.

2. Position desired trim on each bell center and edge stitch in place. Trim ends even with edge of bell centers.

Make 5.

3. For each bell make a set of side pieces using two 2½" x 6½" Fabric B pieces and two 1½" Fabric A squares and following Quick Corner Triangles directions on page 138.

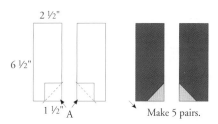

Make 5 pairs.

4. Sew side pieces to each bell center. Press seams toward side pieces.

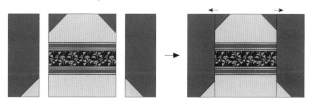

5. Sew a 2½" x 4½" Fabric B piece to each long edge of 1½" x 2½" Fabric A piece for each bell.

Make 5.

6. Sew a 3½" x 9½" Fabric B piece to bottom edge of each bell. Press seams toward Fabric A. Add pieces made in step 5 to top edges of bells, carefully matching fabrics. Block will measure 9½" x 11½".

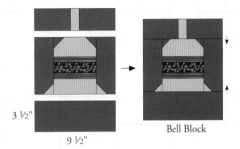

3 ½"

9 ½"

Bell Block

7. Arrange bell blocks side-by-side and sew together. Press seams in one direction. Add optional narrow trims to bottom edge of one or more bells, turning under raw ends even with ends of bottom edge of bell.

8. Sew short ends of 2½" x 40" and 2½" x 10" Fabric B sashing strips together; repeat with 6½" strips for mantel cover top. Press seams to one side. Measure top edge of quilt and cut these strips the same length. Sew the two strips together, placing joining seams at opposite ends.

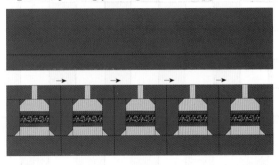

9. Sew edge of sashing unit to top edge of strip of bells.

10. Use bell-handle circle pattern on page 53 and Quick Fuse following directions page 139; **or** trace circle onto wrong side of each bell fabric and cut out with ¼" seam allowance all around to hand appliqué. Turn under ¼" and baste. Appliqué handle to each bell.

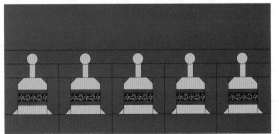

LAYERING AND FINISHING

1. Sew 7½" x 23" backing strip to short end of longer backing strip. Press seam to one side. Place batting on flat surface with backing on top, right side up.

2. On wrong side of pieced mantel cover, place edge of scallop template (see page 53) and draw line ¼" above bottom raw edge of cover. This is the stitching line. Center mantel cover on backing and batting and baste (see step 3 of Layering the Quilt on page 138). Stitch through all layers, stitching on scalloped lines and leaving a 6"-long opening along upper edge for turning. Clip corners and trim excess batting and backing even with cover. Trim excess fabric and batting layers at bottom edge, leaving a ¼"-wide seam allowance beyond stitching.

Batting   Right side of backing

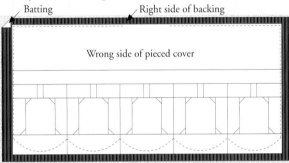

Wrong side of pieced cover

3. Turn mantel cover right side out through opening. Turn opening edges under, press, and slipstitch together by hand.

4. Baste then machine or hand quilt as desired.

5. Sew a smaller button to each bell handle and a larger button to bottom of each bell for clapper.

6. Hand sew beaded fringe trim to lower scalloped edge.

SOMETHING MORE

It's easy to customize this design to fit your mantel. Just add more blocks! Each finished block measures 9" x 11". Before adding the sashing strip above the strip of bells, adjust the measurements of the sashing, backing, and batting pieces to fit your row of bell blocks.

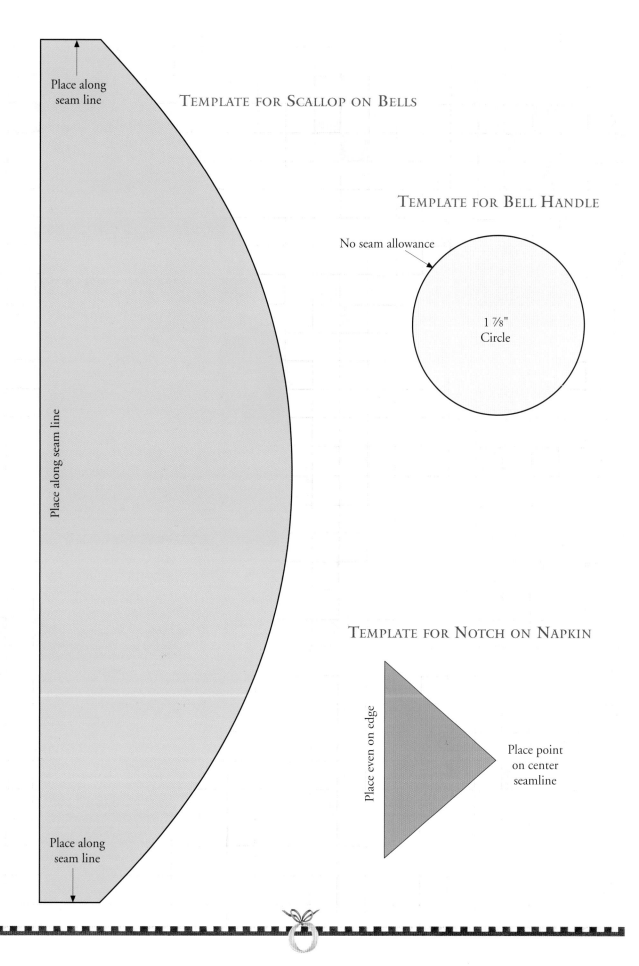

Place along
seam line

TEMPLATE FOR SCALLOP ON BELLS

TEMPLATE FOR BELL HANDLE

No seam allowance

1 ⅞"
Circle

Place along seam line

TEMPLATE FOR NOTCH ON NAPKIN

Place even on edge

Place point
on center
seamline

Place along
seam line

VELVET NAPKIN RINGS

For the ultimate in elegant touches, add a bit of jewels and velvet to your holiday table. These quick and easy velvet napkin rings are finished with gold and glittering buttons from an antique store ... or choose from your own collection.

FABRIC REQUIREMENTS

Velvet - ¼ yard
(*makes four*)
Buttons
Four large and ornate
(1½"-2" diameter)

MAKING THE NAPKIN RINGS

1. From velvet, cut two 4½" x 42" strips. Cut into four 4½" x 15½" pieces.
2. Fold each fabric strip in half lengthwise and stitch ¼" from long raw edges, leaving 2" opening for turning. Center the seam in the strip, finger press lightly and use template on page 53 to mark ends for stitching. Stitch ¼" from drawn lines, pivoting at centered seam. Trim excess velvet. Clip across points and turn right side out. Hand stitch opening closed.
3. Make two 1¼"-long machine buttonholes, beginning each one 4" from one end and ¼" from folded edge. Cut open carefully.

4"

4. Center a large decorative button between buttonholes and sew in place.
5. To use napkin rings, center folded napkin on wrong side of velvet strip. Bring one end over napkin and insert from top through one buttonhole; bring it up through second buttonhole and draw up around napkin.

GOLDEN PEAR PLACE CARD AND HOLDER

For more pizzazz at your Christmas table, add more gold! Create these golden pears to hold the place cards you've lettered … with gold ink, of course!

MATERIALS NEEDED

PLACE CARD HOLDER

Wooden pears - *(approximately 3½" tall, not including stem)*
Small handsaw
Acrylic craft paint - black
Gold leaf adhesive
Old paintbrush
Gold leaf
Gold foil tooling for leaf
Old scissors
Embossing tool
Old toothbrush
Spray matte varnish
Antiquing medium
Fine-gauge rusty wire
Leather or suede shoestring
   cut into 1" pieces for
   pear stems
Glue

PLACE CARD

Cardstock - ivory-colored
Checkerboard rubber stamp
Embossing powder - gold
Embossing ink - gold
Ink pen - black or gold

MAKING THE PLACE CARD HOLDERS

Before you begin, read Painting Techniques on page 139.

1. Using small handsaw, make a ¼"-deep slit toward front of each wooden pear.

Make ¼" deep cut

2. Paint pears black. Allow to dry.
3. Using old paintbrush, apply an even coat of gold leaf adhesive to one pear. Allow to dry until clear.
4. Apply gold leaf to pear following manufacturer's directions. Repeat steps 2 and 3 with remaining pears.
5. Using old scissors, cut leaf shape for each pear from gold foil tooling. Create a vein in center of each leaf with embossing tool.

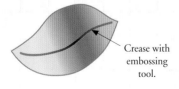

Crease with embossing tool.

6. Referring to Painting Techniques on page 139, spatter pears and leaves with black paint. Allow to dry.
7. Spray pears and leaves with matte varnish. Allow to dry.
8. Following manufacturer's directions, apply antiquing medium to pears and leaves. Allow to dry. Add finish coat of varnish.
9. Cut a 4"-long piece of rusty wire for each pear. Wrap around a pencil to curl and slip off. Make a small hole in each leaf and attach one end of wire. Wrap end around pear stem and glue stem to top of pear. Crimp leaf.

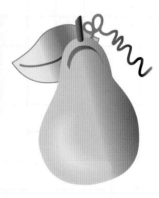

10. Slip a pretty place card into the slit in each pear.

MAKING THE CARDS

1. Cut cardstock into desired number of 2" x 3½" cards.
2. Use rubber stamp and gold embossing ink to create checkerboard at top edge of card.
3. Sprinkle gold embossing powder on checkerboard and heat with gun or blow dryer on low setting.
4. Write guests' names on cards in black or gold ink.
5. Tuck each card into the slit at top of Golden Pear place card holders.

QUICK START

You can purchase sheets of perforated business card stock designed for computer printers at an office supply store. No cutting necessary! Just separate the cards and emboss!

CHRISTMAS DINNER

The flicker of candlelight, soft notes of familiar Christmas carols and the sparkle of your very best china … the perfect setting for a magical Christmas dinner, five elegant courses to celebrate the Fifth Day of Christmas. With our deliciously festive menu and recipes, your Christmas feast will be an event to remember! A delicious menu and the recipes are easy to follow.

MUSHROOM SOUP

STEAMED MUSSELS WITH PESTO
ON TOAST POINTS

CLASSIC CHRISTMAS SALAD

ROASTED GAME HEN
WITH SWEET POTATO STUFFING

BRAISED BRUSSELS SPROUTS OR CABBAGE

MAPLE BUTTER

POACHED PEARS WITH CRÉME ANGLAISE
AND STUFFED WITH CHOCOLATE GANACHE

FLORENTINE COOKIES

Steamed Mussels with Pesto on Toast Points

SERVES 12

1 SMALL HEAD GARLIC

1 BUNCH BASIL, LEAVES ONLY

¼ CUP PINE NUTS OR PEANUTS (OPTIONAL)

¼ CUP OLIVE OIL

1 CUP WHITE WINE

1 TOMATO, PEELED, SEEDED, AND DICED

3 SPRIGS THYME OR A TEASPOON DRIED THYME LEAVES

5 SPRIGS PARSLEY OR 1 TABLESPOON DRIED PARSLEY

1 BAY LEAF

1 TABLESPOON CHOPPED CHIVES (OPTIONAL)

1 LEMON, JUICED OR 2 TABLESPOONS

PINCH SALT AND PEPPER

MUSSELS (1½ LBS. FOR 12 PEOPLE)

6 SLICES BREAD, TOASTED AND CUT INTO TRIANGLES, UNBUTTERED

PESTO: *Break up the head of garlic and peel. Save three of the cloves for the steamed mussels.*
Use the rest in the pesto. For stronger garlic flavor in the pesto, use a larger garlic head or more cloves. Place basil leaves, garlic, pine nuts, and olive oil into a blender. Pulse to a paste. Scrape the sides regularly and add a pinch of salt. Transfer to a serving dish and set aside.

Preparing Mussels: *Pull off the beards. Place the white wine, tomato, herbs, garlic, lemon juice, and salt and pepper into a large pot and bring to a boil. Reduce heat to medium and add mussels. Cover. Cook until mussels pop open (about five minutes). Drain. Serve immediately with pesto and toasted bread.*

Mushroom Soup

SERVES 12

OIL, FOR SAUTÉ

1 SMALL ONION, DICED

2 CARROTS, DICED

2 STICKS CELERY, DICED

3 CLOVES GARLIC, MINCED

1 SHALLOT, MINCED

3 SPRIGS THYME, CHOPPED

1 BAY LEAF

3 SPRIGS PARSLEY, CHOPPED

1 SPRIG ROSEMARY, CHOPPED

1 LB. ASSORTED MUSHROOMS

1 QT. CHICKEN STOCK

SALT AND PEPPER

METHOD: *Heat oil in a skillet and sauté the onion, carrot, and celery until almost tender. Add the garlic, shallot, and herbs. Cook until shallot is translucent. Add mushrooms and stock and bring to a boil. Salt and pepper to taste. Reduce heat and simmer for 30 minutes. Remove bay leaf before serving.*

ROASTED GAME HEN WITH SWEET POTATO STUFFING

SERVES 12

12 GAME HENS	½ TEASPOON PAPRIKA
1 APPLE	½ TEASPOON BLACK
3 SLICES BACON	PEPPER
6 SMALL SWEET POTATOES	1 TEASPOON SALT
1 SMALL ONION	¼ CUP PECANS
BUTTER, FOR SAUTÉ	¼ CUP RAISINS
½ TEASPOON CINNAMON	

METHOD: *Wash, dry, and trim off any excess skin from the hens. Cut the apple, bacon, sweet potato, and onion into small bite-size pieces. Heat a large skillet to medium-low, add bacon and cook. Add the apple and onion and cook until juice starts to come out of the apple. Turn up heat slightly and add sweet potato. Sauté until sweet potato begins to cook. Add more butter if needed. Add spices, pecans, and raisins and cook until hot. Set aside a quarter of the stuffing for garnish. Stuffing needs to be fully chilled before stuffing the hens.*

Preheat oven to 375°F. Stuff the game hens with chilled stuffing. Brush each with the maple butter (see recipe on following page). Place in a 9" x 13" pan and bake, basting with the maple butter until the temperature reaches 145 -160°F on a meat thermometer.

CLASSIC CHRISTMAS SALAD

SERVES 12

1 RUBY RED GRAPEFRUIT	¼ TEASPOON SALT
1 NAVEL ORANGE	¼ TEASPOON BLACK
1 BLOOD ORANGE OR	PEPPER
HONEY TANGERINE	1 CUP OLIVE OIL
½ SHALLOT	LETTUCE MIX - ICEBERG,
⅓ CUP WHITE WINE	RED LEAF, ROMAINE,
VINEGAR	SPRING MIX

METHOD: *Peel and section the grapefruit and oranges. Cut each section into small pieces. Mince the shallot. Place the vinegar, salt, pepper, and shallot into a small bowl. Whisk in olive oil. Add the grapefruit and oranges.*

The dressing will be best if allowed to sit overnight, but not necessary. Just before serving, let dressing come to room temperature, mix, and serve over the lettuce.

BRAISED BRUSSELS SPROUTS OR CABBAGE

SERVES 12

3 SLICES BACON, CUT

1 SMALL ONION,
DICED SMALL

1 SMALL GRANNY SMITH
APPLE, PEELED, CORED,
AND DICED SMALL

½ CUP WATER

1 TABLESPOON WHITE
WINE VINEGAR

2 TABLESPOONS
WHITE WINE

2 TABLESPOONS SUGAR

1 CINNAMON STICK

1 WHOLE CLOVE

3 JUNIPER BERRIES
(OPTIONAL)

1 BAY LEAF

1 LB. BRUSSELS SPROUTS
OR CABBAGE

SALT AND PEPPER

METHOD: *In a large skillet, cook the bacon at very low heat. Sauté the onion and the apple together with the bacon. Add the water, vinegar, white wine, sugar, and spices. Add the Brussels sprouts or the cabbage and braise at 325°F until the sprouts are tender or the cabbage is cooked through. Season with salt and pepper and remove the loose spices.*

MAPLE BUTTER

SERVES 12

1 STICK BUTTER,
SOFTENED

3 TABLESPOONS
MAPLE SYRUP

METHOD: *Place softened butter in mixer bowl. Whip until fluffy. Add maple syrup one tablespoon at a time, scraping the bowl after each addition, until syrup is incorporated.*

POACHED PEARS WITH CRÈME ANGLAISE, STUFFED WITH CHOCOLATE GANACHE

SERVES 4-8

THE POACHED PEARS:

- 1 (750ML.) BOTTLE RED WINE OR PORT
- 2 CUPS SUGAR
- 1 STICK CINNAMON
- 1 GINGER ROOT
- ½ VANILLA BEAN OR 1 TEASPOON VANILLA EXTRACT
- 5 CLOVES
- PEARS (2 FOR FOUR PEOPLE, 3 FOR SIX, AND 4 FOR EIGHT PEOPLE)

THE CRÈME ANGLAISE:

- 3 EGG YOLKS
- ¼ CUP SUGAR
- 1 CUP MILK
- ½ VANILLA BEAN OR 1 TEASPOON VANILLA EXTRACT

THE CHOCOLATE GANACHE:

- 1 CUP CREAM
- 8 OZ. CHOCOLATE CHIPS, SEMI-SWEET OR MILK CHOCOLATE

METHOD: *For the pears, peel and cut each pear in half, taking care that each half includes half of the stem. Using a melon baller or small knife, remove the seeds. Core with a melon baller. Place all the ingredients except the pears into a stainless steel pan and bring to a boil. Reduce heat to a simmer. Put in the pears, and add water if needed to completely cover. There should be big, lazy bubbles coming from the bottom of pan.*

For the crème, whip the egg yolks and sugar until sugar is dissolved and you can make a ribbon with the yolks. Scald the milk. Slowly pour over egg yolk mixture while still beating the yolks. Scrape in the vanilla bean or add extract. Beat mixture over hot water until thick, taking care not to scramble the eggs. Serve warm.

For the ganache, in a saucepan, scald the cream. Pour over chocolate chips. Stir to make sure all the chocolate is melted. Let sit until it sets up, or overnight.

FLORENTINE COOKIES

YIELDS 24

1 CUP PACKED BROWN SUGAR	¾ CUP FLOUR
1 STICK PLUS 1 TABLE-SPOON OF BUTTER	¼ CUP OATMEAL
½ CUP CORN SYRUP	½ CUP SLIVERED ALMONDS

METHOD: *In a heavy bottom pot, bring the first three ingredients to a boil. Remove from heat and add the remaining ingredients. Scrape into a heat-proof container and let cool completely. Roll into balls and press into circles on parchment or wax paper that has been pan-sprayed and placed on a cookie sheet that has been turned upside down. Bake in a pre-heated 375°F oven until they stop bubbling. Take care not to overcook. While the cookies are still hot, you can have fun bending them into different shapes.*

SIX GEESE-A-LAYING

SIX GEESE-A-LAYING

On the sixth day of Christmas
my true love sent to me,
Six Geese-a-Laying ...

*The traditional Christmas goose …
what a familiar favorite of the season. His
country warmth and charm will add that special
touch to your gift giving and holiday home.*

SIX GEESE-A-LAYING QUILT

What a perfect gift for your own true love … this six geese-a-laying quilt you've joyously created. Its country elegance can be enjoyed even after the holiday season too.

Finished Size: 87" x 96"
Finished Block: 13" x 19"

FABRIC REQUIREMENTS

Fabric A (*goose background, vines, and flower blocks*) - 3½ yards

Fabric B (*goose body*) - ¾ yard

Fabric C (*goose neck and head*) - ½ yard

Fabric D (*upper wing feathers*) - ⅙ yard

Fabric E (*middle wing feathers*) - ¼ yard

Fabric F (*lower wing feathers*) - ⅙ yard

Fabric G (*white for neck*) - ⅛ yard

Fabric H (*beak*) - ⅛ yard

Fabric I (*red lattice around blocks*) ⅝ yard

Fabric J (*dark green flying geese triangles and vines*) - 4 yards of one print or ½ yard each of eleven greens

Fabric K (*light green flying geese corner triangles*) - 2⅜ yards

Fabric L (*light tan accent borders 3 and 5*) - 1⅙ yards

Fabric M (*red for flowers*) - ½ yard

Fabric N (*black for flowers*) ¼ yard

Fabric O (*tan for flowers*) ⅙ yard

First accent border (*black*) ⅓ yard

Second accent border (*red*) ⅝ yard

Backing - 8 yards

Batting - 96" x 104" piece

Binding - ⅞ yard

CUTTING THE STRIPS AND PIECES

Read first paragraph of Cutting the Strips and Pieces on page 14.

Fabric A (*goose background, vines, and flower blocks*)

One 6½" x 42" strip, cut into
- Six 6½" squares

One 5½" x 42" strip, cut into
- Six 5½" squares

One 3½" x 24" strip, cut into
- Six 3½" squares

Three 2½" x 42" strips, cut into
- Twenty-four 2½" squares
- Six 2½" x 5½" pieces

Four 1½" x 42" strips, cut into
- Six 1½" x 6½" pieces
- Six 1½" x 4½" pieces
- Six 1½" x 3½" pieces
- Six 1½" x 2½" pieces
- Thirty 1½" squares

Sixteen 3½" x 42" strips, cut into
- Ninety 3½" x 6½" rectangles for vines
- Eight 3½" squares for vines

Four 3" x 42" strips, cut into
- Sixteen 3" x 5½" rectangles for flowers
- Sixteen 3" squares for flowers

Fabric B (*goose body*)

One 7½" x 42" strip, cut into
- Six 5½" x 7½" pieces

Four 2½" x 42" strips, cut into
- Six 2½" x 12½" pieces
- Thirty 2½" squares

Two 1½" x 42" strips, cut into
- Twenty-four 1½" squares
- Six 1½" x 4½" pieces
- Six 1½" x 2½" pieces

Fabric C (*neck and head*)

One 5½" x 42" strip, cut into
- Six 5½" x 6½" pieces

One 2½" x 42" strip, cut into
- Six 2½" x 5½" pieces

Two 1½" x 42" strips, cut into
- Twelve 1½" x 2½" pieces
- Twelve 1½" squares

Fabric D (*top wing feathers*)

Three 1½" x 42" strips, cut into
- Six 1½" x 7½" pieces
- Six 1½" x 10½" pieces
- Six 1½" squares

Fabric E (*middle wing feathers*)

Two 2½" x 42" strips, cut into
- Six 2½" x 12½" pieces

Fabric F (*lower wing feathers*)

Two 2½" x 42" strips, cut into
- Six 2½" x 11½" pieces

Fabric G (*white neck accent*)

One 1½" x 42" strip, cut into
- Six 1½" x 2½" pieces
- Six 1½" squares

Fabric H (*beak*)

One 1½" x 20" strip, cut into
- Twelve 1½" squares

Fabric I (*red lattice around blocks*)

Twelve 1½" x 42" strips, cut into*
- Twelve 1½" x 15½" pieces
- Twelve 1½" x 19½" pieces
- * Cut one 15½" and one 19½" strip from each 42" strip

Fabric J (*dark green*)

Twenty-one 3½" x 42" strips, cut into
- One hundred twenty-five 3½" x 6½" rectangles for flying geese

Eighteen 3½" x 42" strips, cut into
- One hundred eighty-eight 3½" squares for vines

Fabric K (*light green*)

Twenty-three 3½" x 42" strips, cut into
- Two hundred fifty 3½" squares for flying geese corner triangles

Fabric L (*tan for accent borders 3 and 5*)

Fifteen 2½" x 42" strips

Fabric M (*red for flowers*)

One 5½" x 42" strip cut into
- Four 5½" squares

Three 3" x 42" strips cut into
- Thirty-two 3" squares

Fabric N (*black for flowers*)

Four 5½" circles

Fabric O (*tan for flowers*)

Four 5" circles

First Accent Border (*black*)

Seven 1½" x 42" strips

Second Accent Border (*red*)

Seven 2½" x 42" strips

Binding - Ten 2¼" x 42" strips

TIP

You will be cutting many pieces for this big quilt. To keep them organized, store them in clear plastic self-sealing bags according to the fabric and how they are used in the quilt. For example, you'll need three bags for Fabric A. Use one for the goose background pieces, one for the vine pieces, and one for the flower block pieces. Label each bag so it's easy to grab the one you need.

MAKING THE GOOSE BLOCKS AND FLYING GEESE LATTICE

1. Make six goose blocks, following directions for wall hanging on pages 70-72.

2. Sew a 1½" x 19½" Fabric I lattice strip to top and bottom edges of each block. Press seams toward lattice. Sew a 1½" x 15½" Fabric I lattice strip to each side of each goose block.

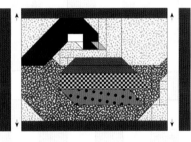

3. Make one hundred twenty-five flying geese units, using 3½" x 6½" Fabric J pieces and 3½" Fabric K squares.

Make 125.

4. Sew flying geese units together in groups of seven units each to make eight lattice strips. Press seams toward long edge of green triangle in each unit. Sew remaining flying geese units together to make three strips of twenty-three units each.

5. Referring to the quilt layout, arrange goose blocks in two rows of three blocks each with eight short lattice strips. Sew together, making sure the flying geese are pointing in the correct direction. Press seams toward goose blocks.

6. Sew long lattice strips to rows of blocks, positioning strips so geese are pointing in the correct direction.

7. Cut one strip of 1½"-wide first accent border in half; sew halves to two first accent border strips. Measure quilt through center from side-to-side and trim two strips to this measurement. Sew to top and bottom edges of quilt top.

8. Sew remaining first accent border strips together in pairs. Measure quilt top through center from top to bottom. Trim strips to this measurement. Sew strips to sides of quilt.

9. Repeat steps 7 and 8 to attach second accent border.

MAKING THE VINE BORDER

You will make three different units for these borders.

1. Referring to Quick-Corner Triangles on page 138, make units A, B, and C, using 3½" x 6½" Fabric A rectangles and 3½" Fabric J squares. Press.

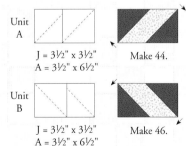

Unit A
J = 3½" x 3½"
A = 3½" x 6½"
Make 44.

Unit B
J = 3½" x 3½"
A = 3½" x 6½"
Make 46.

Sew 3½" Fabric A squares to 3½" Fabric J squares. Press.

Unit C
J = 3½" x 3½"
A = 3½" x 3½"
Make 8.

2. Make top and bottom border strips, arranging vines and squares as shown in diagram. Each border requires ten of Unit A with a Unit C at opposite ends and eleven of Unit B.

Unit B

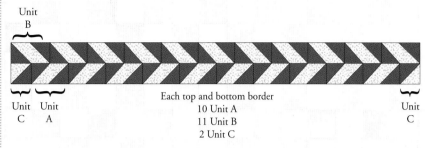

Unit C   Unit A

Each top and bottom border
10 Unit A
11 Unit B
2 Unit C

Unit C

3. Make side borders using twelve of Unit A, twelve of Unit B, and two of Unit C in each vine strip.

Unit C   Unit A

Unit B

Each side border
12 Unit A
12 Unit B

Unit C

4. Sew eight of the 2½"-wide Fabric L border strips together in pairs; cut one 2½" x 75½" strip from each pair for a total of four strips. Sew the remaining seven 2½"-wide border strips together to make one long piece. Cut four 2½" x 66½" strips from the long strip.

5. Sew Fabric L border strips to both sides of long edges of each vine border.

MAKING THE FLOWER BLOCKS AND ADDING VINE BORDERS

1. Referring to page 66, step 3, make sixteen flying geese units with the Quick Corner Triangle technique, using 3" x 5½" Fabric A pieces and 3" Fabric M squares. Press.

2. Sew 3" Fabric A squares to opposite ends of eight flying geese units from step 1. Press.

3. Sew two of remaining units from step 1 to opposite sides of each 5½" Fabric M square. Press. Make four.

Make 4.

4. Sew units from steps 2 and 3 together to make four flower blocks.

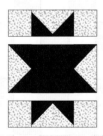

Make 4.

5. Referring to Hand Appliqué directions on page 138, appliqué 5½" Fabric M circle to center of each star block. Hand appliqué 5" Fabric N circle in center of Fabric M circle on each block.

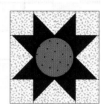

Make 4.

6. Sew a Flower Block to both ends of each short vine border. Press.

7. Sew a long vine border to sides of quilt top. Press. Add top and bottom vine borders with flowers. Press.

LAYERING AND FINISHING

1. Cut backing crosswise into three 42" x 96" strips. Sew long edges together to make one 96" x 126" piece. Trim to 96" x 104".

2. Arrange and baste backing, batting, and quilt top together, referring to Layering the Quilt on page 138.

3. Machine or hand quilt as desired.

4. Bind quilt referring to Binding the Quilt on page 139.

SIX GEESE-A-LAYING PILLOWCASE

Fabric Needed

(for one pillowcase)

Flying Geese Block

Six assorted dark green fabrics 3½" x 6½"

Six assorted light green fabrics cut twelve 3½" squares

Cutting and Assembly

Trim

Cut one 1½" x 20½"

Cut two 6½" x 1½"

Cut one 9½" x 20½"

Cut one 16½" x 20½"

Main Fabric

Cut two 22½" x 20½"

1. Make six flying geese blocks following instructions on page 66. Sew into a strip unit. Unit measures 6½" x 18½".

2. Sew 6½" x 1½" trim to top and bottom of above unit.

3. 1½" x 20½" trim is sewn to the left side of Flying Geese unit. Points face toward the top.

4. Sew 9½" x 20½" strip to the right of above unit. Press toward the trim.

5. Place pieced unit and 16½" x 20½" fabric right sides together. Sew along 16½" sides. Press.

6. Fold in half placing raw edges together. Press. Width measures 8½".

7. Place right sides of main fabric together and sew along edges leaving one 20½" side open.

8. Sew pieced unit from step 6 to main fabric and press. Finished size is 30" x 20".

CHRISTMAS GOOSE WALL QUILT

*In honor of that star of
the holiday feast — the
Christmas Goose — create
this inviting holiday
wallhanging. Or make it
in colors to coordinate with
your décor and enjoy
its country charm
throughout the year.*

Finished Size: 28" x 34"

FABRIC REQUIREMENTS

Fabric A - (*background*)
⅜ yard

Fabric B - (*body*) ⅓ yard

Fabric C - (*neck and head*)
⅙ yard

Fabric D - (*top wing feather*)
⅛ yard or a scrap

Fabric E - (*middle wing feather*)
⅛ yard or a scrap

Fabric F - (*bottom wing feather*)
⅛ yard or a scrap

Fabric G - (*white for neck*) scrap

Fabric H - (*beak*) scrap

Fabric I - (*red flying geese
triangles*) ¼ yard each of
five different fabrics

Fabric J - (*tan flying geese
background*) ⅔ yard

Accent border - ⅛ yard

Backing - 1 yard

Batting - 32" x 38" piece

Binding - ⅜ yard

CUTTING THE STRIPS AND PIECES

*Read first paragraph of Cutting
the Strips and Pieces on page 14.*

Fabric A (*background*)

One 6½" square

One 5½" square

One 3½" square

One 1½" x 42" strip, cut into
- One 1½" x 6½" piece
- One 1½" x 4½" piece
- One 1½" x 2½" piece
- One 1½" x 3½" piece
- Five 1½" squares

One 2½" x 42" strip, cut into
- Four 2½" squares
- One 2½" x 5½" piece

MAKING THE GOOSE HEAD

PIECING THE BLOCKS

Many of the steps in the following pages require quick corner-triangle units. Refer to Quick Corner Triangle directions on pages 138 for making these units.

1. Using a 2½" square of Fabric A and Fabric B, make a quick corner triangle unit, trim, and press. On wrong side of unit, draw a diagonal line as shown in diagram.

Sewing line

Fabric B (*goose body*)

One 5½" x 7½" piece
One 2½" x 42" strip, cut into
  • One 2½" x 12½" piece
  • Five 2½" squares
One 1½" x 42" strip, cut into
  • Four 1½" squares
  • One 1½" x 2½" piece
  • One 1½" x 4½" piece

Fabric C (*neck and head*)
  • One 5½" x 6½" piece
  • One 2½" x 5½" piece
One 1½" x 42" strip, cut into
  • Two 1½" x 2½" pieces
  • Two 1 ½" squares

Fabric D (*top wing feathers*)
One 1½" x 7½" strip
One 1½" x 10½" strip
One 1½" square

Fabric E (*middle wing feathers*)
One 2½" x 12½" strip

Fabric F (*bottom wing feathers*)
One 2½" x 11½" strip

Fabric G (*white for neck*)
One 1½" x 2½" piece
One 1½" square

Fabric H (*beak*)
Two 1½" squares

Fabric I (*red flying geese triangles*)
Seven 3½" x 6½" pieces from each of five different fabrics

Fabric J (*tan flying geese background*)
Six 3½" x 42" strips, cut into
  • Sixty-four 3½" squares

Accent border - Two 1½" x 42" strips, cut into
  • Two 1½" x 19½" strips
  • Two 1½" x 15½" strips

Backing - One 32" x 38" piece

Binding - Four 2¾" x 42" strips

2. Paying careful attention to direction of drawn line, position square face down in lower right corner of 5½" x 6½" Fabric C piece. Stitch on drawn line, trim, and press.

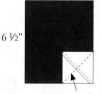

5 ½"

6 ½"

Sewing line

3. Sew 5½" Fabric A square to upper left corner of unit from step 2. Press.

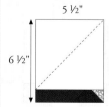

5 ½"

6 ½"

4. Make a quick corner triangle, using 2½" Fabric A square and 2½" x 5½" Fabric C piece. Press.

5. Sew 1½" Fabric C square and 1½" x 2½" piece of Fabric C to opposite ends of 1½" x 2½" Fabric G piece. Press.

6. Make quick corner triangles, using 1½" Fabric C square, 1½" x 3½" Fabric A piece, and 1½" Fabric G square. Press.

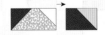

7. Make quick corner triangles, using 1½" x 2½" Fabric C piece and 1½" Fabric H square.

8. Sew unit from step 7 to short end of unit made in step 6.

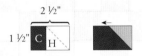

9. Sew together units made in steps 5-8. Press.

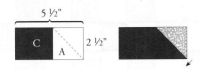

10. Make quick corner triangle, using 1½" x 4½" Fabric A piece and remaining 1½" Fabric H square. Press.

11. Sew step 10 unit to right edge of head unit from step 9.

12. Sew 1½" x 6½" Fabric A strip to bottom edge of head unit. Press.

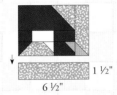

13. Sew 2½" x 5½" Fabric A piece to right edge of head unit. Press.

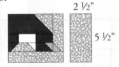

14. Make a quick corner triangle, using 1½" x 7½" Fabric D piece and 1½" Fabric A square.

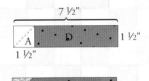

15. Sew 1½" Fabric A square to triangle end of strip from step 14.

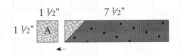

16. Sew strip from step 15 to bottom edge of head unit.

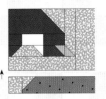

17. Make quick corner triangles at each lower corner of 6½" Fabric A square using one 1½" Fabric B square and one 1½" Fabric D square.

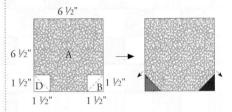

18. Referring to quilt layout on page 70, sew neck and head units from steps 3 and 16 together. Add unit from step 17. Press.

MAKING THE GOOSE BODY

1. Make quick corner triangle, using 5½" x 7½" Fabric B piece and 3½" Fabric A square. Trim and press.

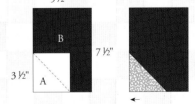

2. Make quick corner triangles at each end of 1½" x 10½" Fabric D strip, using two 1½" Fabric B squares. Press.

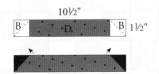

3. Sew a 1½" x 4½" Fabric B strip to right end. Press.

4. Make a quick corner triangle at right end of 2½" x 12½" Fabric E strip, using 2½" Fabric B square. Press.

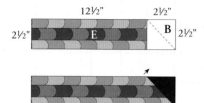

5. Make a quick corner triangle at right end of 1½" x 2½" Fabric B piece, using 1½" Fabric A square. Press.

6. Sew together 1½" Fabric A and B squares. Sew to bottom edge of unit made in step 5.

7. Make quick corner triangles at short ends of 2½" x 11½" Fabric F strip, using a 2½" Fabric B square at lower left corner and 2½" Fabric B square at upper right corner. Press.

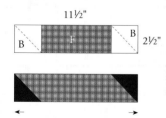

8. Make a quick corner triangle unit with 1½" square Fabric A and 2½" Fabric B square.

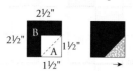

9. Sew units from steps 7 and 8 together, adding a 1½" x 2½" Fabric A piece at right end. Press.

10. Make a quick corner triangle at right end of 2½" x 12½" Fabric B strip with 2½" Fabric A square. Press.

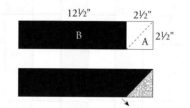

11. Add remaining 2½" Fabric A square to right end of unit made in step 10.

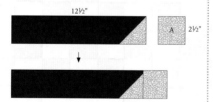

12. Arrange strips for goose body in order and sew together. Press.

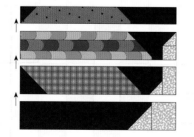

13. Sew unit from step 1 to left edge of unit from step 12.

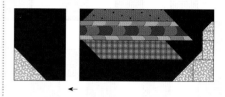

14. Sew goose head to goose body. Press.

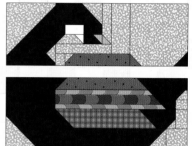

Block measures 19½" x 13½".

Making the Flying Geese Border

1. For each flying goose block, sew one 3½" Fabric J square to 3½" x 6½" Fabric I piece. Press.

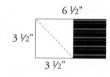

2. Sew a 3½" Fabric J square to unit from step 1. Press. Make a total of thirty-two flying geese.

Make 32.

3. Referring to quilt photo and paying attention to direction geese are pointing, arrange flying geese blocks around quilt top in desired order. Sew nine flying geese units together for each side border and seven flying geese units together for top and bottom borders. Press seams in each strip toward bottom edge of large triangles. Do not sew to quilt yet.

ASSEMBLY

1. Sew 1½" x 19½" accent borders to top and bottom of goose block. Press seams toward border.
2. Sew 1½" x 15½" accent borders to sides of goose block. Press seams toward border.
3. Referring to layout on page 70, sew flying geese border strips to top and bottom edges of quilt top with geese pointing in correct direction. Press toward accent border. Add side borders and press.

LAYERING AND FINISHING

1. Arrange and baste backing, batting, and quilt top together, referring to Layering the Quilt on page 138.
2. Machine or hand quilt as desired.
3. Bind quilt referring to Binding the Quilt on page 139.

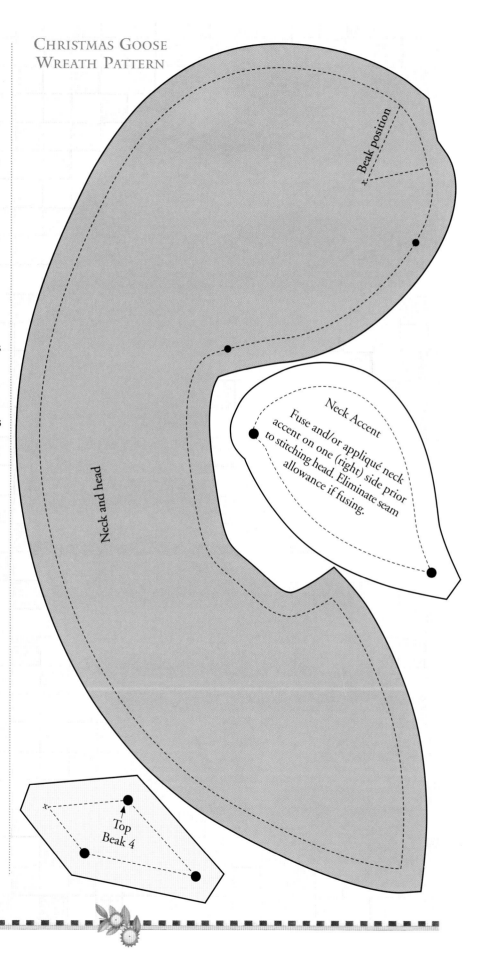

CHRISTMAS GOOSE
WREATH PATTERN

Beak position

Neck and head

Neck Accent
Fuse and/or appliqué neck accent on one (right) side prior to stitching head. Eliminate seam allowance if fusing.

Top
Beak 4

CHRISTMAS GOOSE WREATH PATTERN

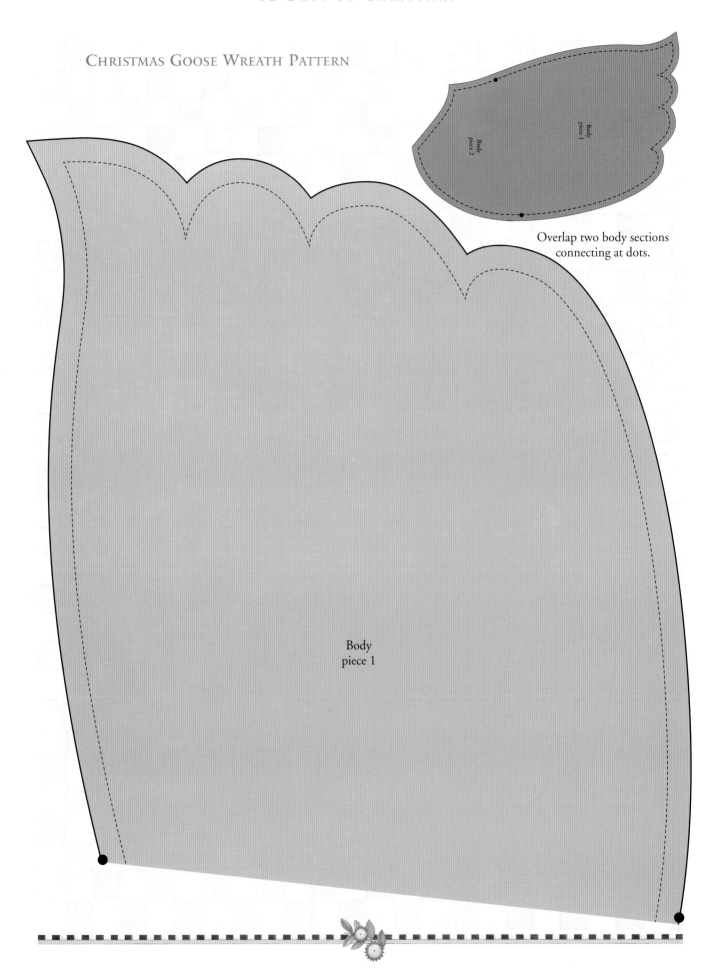

Body
piece 1

Body
piece 2

Overlap two body sections
connecting at dots.

Body
piece 1

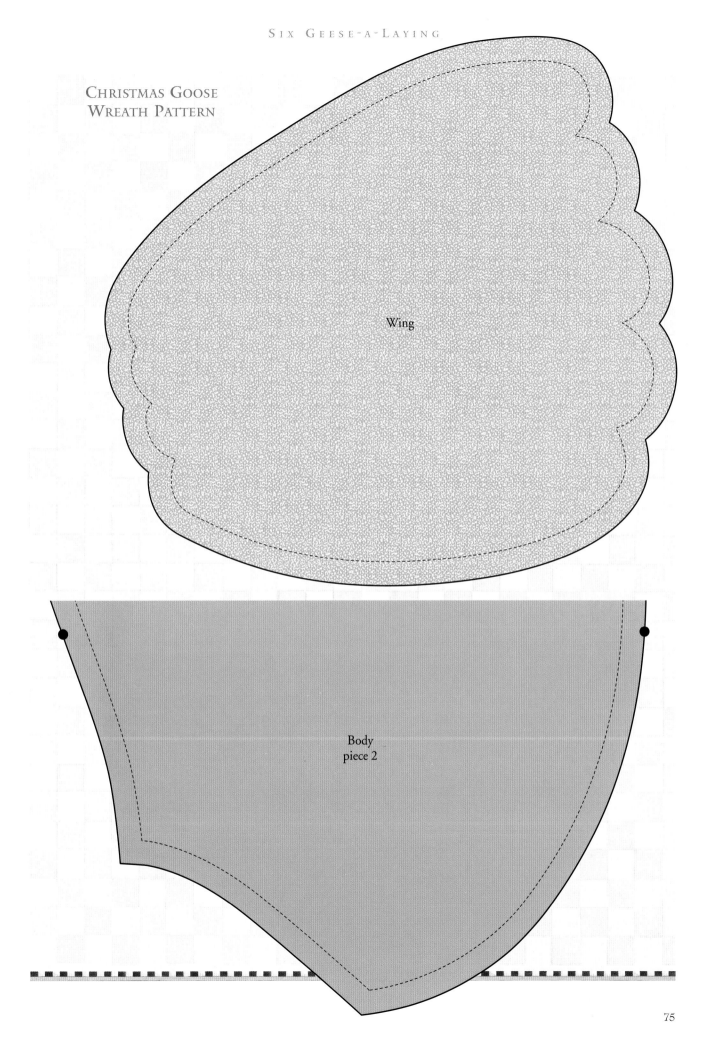

CHRISTMAS GOOSE
WREATH PATTERN

Wing

Body
piece 2

CHRISTMAS GOOSE WREATH

Let this friendly country goose and wreath of fresh evergreens send a warm welcome to holiday guests when they arrive at your front door.

Finished Size: 24" diameter

MATERIALS NEEDED

Houndstooth check wool *(body)* - ¼ yard

Black wool *(neck and head)* 7" x 10" piece

Cream wool *(neck accent)* 3" x 4" piece

Gold wool *(beak)* - 2" x 6" piece

Dark herringbone or plaid wool *(wing)* - 7" x 14"

Lightweight batting 6" x 7" piece

Polyester fiberfill for stuffing

Gold cord - ¼ yard

Buttons - ¼"-diameter white and 1⅛"-diameter black for eye

Perle cotton or embroidery thread - black

Fresh or artificial wreath 24"-diameter

Strong wire 18"-long piece *(neck)* 8"-long piece *(attaching goose to wreath)*

Charms - Six or eight large gold holly leaves or other designs *(about 3½"-long)*

Ribbon - 4 yards, 1¾"-wide

Beads - 4 yards, ³⁄₁₆" diameter

Wired ribbon - 4 yards, 2"-wide

Freezer paper for pattern

Glue gun and glue

MAKING THE GOOSE

1. Trace two of each pattern piece (only one neck accent) on pages 73-75 onto uncoated side of freezer paper. Leave ½" space between pieces and cut each one out on the drawn lines.

2. Press coated side of paper pieces to appropriate fabrics and cut out each wool piece around outside edge of paper. Remove paper.

3. Position cream neck piece on one goose neck and hand or quick fuse appliqué (see page 139) in place.

4. With right sides together, stitch neck to body. Press seam toward body.

5. With right sides together, stitch body pieces together ¼" from raw edges. Leave a 3" opening for turning at bottom edge of body. Clip curves and turn right side out.

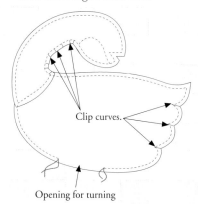

Clip curves.

Opening for turning

6. Bend 18" piece of firm wire in half and tuck into goose neck; surround it with stuffing. Stuff goose (*not too firmly*). Stitch opening closed by hand.

Bent wire

7. With right sides together, stitch beak pieces together from dot to dot to dot. Trim

seams to scant ³⁄₁₆" and turn right side out. Stuff beak lightly. Turn under remaining raw edges and position beak on head. Hand appliqué in place securely.

8. Cut one wing from lightweight batting. Layer wings right sides together on top of batting. Stitch ¼" from raw edges all around.

9. Make small slit in center of one layer of wool wing and turn wing right side out through slit. Press.

10. Using black perle cotton, make large blanket hole stitches around outer edge of wing and stitch feather details with stem stitch. Refer to Embroidery Stitch Guide on page 138. Position wing on goose body and hand tack in place. Add gold cord to neck and tack in place on underside. Stitch buttons in place for eyes with small black button on top.

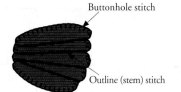

Buttonhole stitch

Outline (stem) stitch

11. Shape goose head as needed, bending wire inside. Tack head to goose body.

Tack beak to body.

ASSEMBLING THE WREATH

1. Referring to the photo on page 76, layer beads on top of 1¾"-wide ribbon, stitch in place and wrap around wreath.

2. Poke 8"-long piece of wire through back of goose body fabric an inch above lower edge and use to attach goose to wreath.

3. Arrange and glue large charms in place with hot glue gun.

4. Make large bow using 2"-wide wired ribbon and attach to wreath below goose.

SOMETHING MORE

Try the goose pattern as an appliqué for a small felted wool pillow. Choose a variety of deep luscious shades of wool, and your goose pillow can become a charming year-round accent.

After tracing your appliqué shapes, buttonhole stitch to layer them together, then stitch the finished goose to another layer of contrasting felted wool.

SEVEN SWANS-A-SWIMMING

SEVEN SWANS A-SWIMMING

On the seventh day of Christmas,
my true love sent to me,
Seven Swans-a-Swimming ...

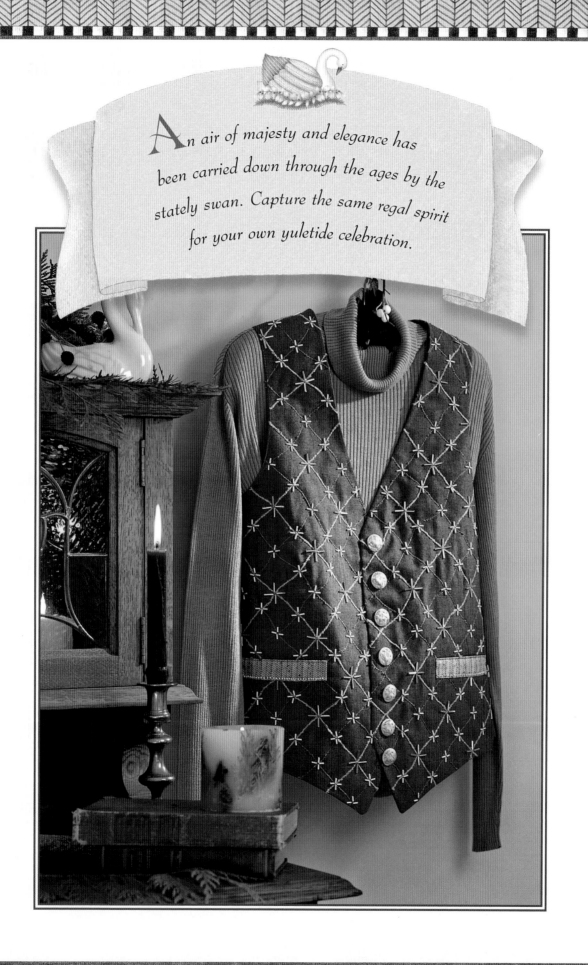

An air of majesty and elegance has been carried down through the ages by the stately swan. Capture the same regal spirit for your own yuletide celebration.

Seven Swans Vest

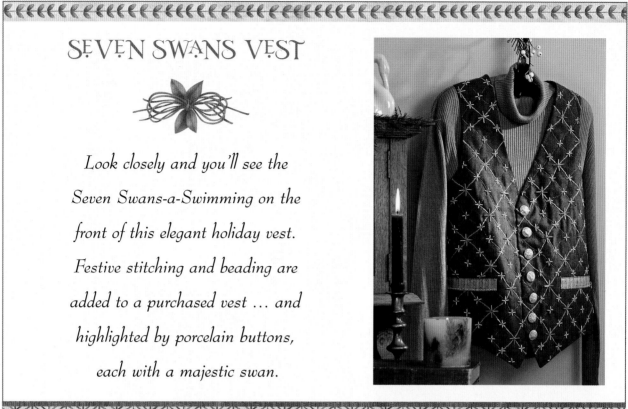

Look closely and you'll see the Seven Swans-a-Swimming on the front of this elegant holiday vest. Festive stitching and beading are added to a purchased vest ... and highlighted by porcelain buttons, each with a majestic swan.

Materials Needed

Purchased vest

Cord or yarn - 10 yards each of two colors, fine gauge decorative

Thread to match cord or yarn

Swans-A-Swimming buttons Seven (*see Ordering Information on page 139*)

Bugle beads - about forty large

Bugle and seed beads - small, in same color

Scrap of fabric for welt pocket

White chalk dressmaker's pencil

Embroidery presser foot

Embellishing the Vest

1. With the vest buttoned so the design will match across the fronts, use dressmaker's chalk pencil and the illustration below to trace the couching design on the vest fronts.

2. Remove original buttons.

3. Using a narrow zigzag stitch and thread to match one of the two decorative yarns, couch it to every other drawn line. Test first on a scrap and adjust zigzag width so it captures the yarn underneath. For best results, use an open-toe embroidery foot so you can see your work. Couch other color yarn on remaining lines. Clip yarns even with vest edges.

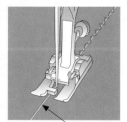

Zigzag over yarn with open-toe embroidery foot.

4. From fabric scrap for welt, cut two 2½" x 5" pieces. The finished welt measures 1" x 4½". If the vest you are using has welt pockets, cut the strips 2½" wide and ½" longer than the welt in the vest.

5. Fold each piece in half lengthwise with right sides together and stitch ¼" from long raw edges, leaving an opening at center for turning. Refold so seam is centered in back of piece and stitch short ends. Clip corners and turn right side out. Press. (It's not necessary to stitch opening closed.)

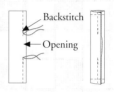

Backstitch

Opening

6. Position welts on vest over any existing welts. Sew to vest by hand or by machine, stitching through vest and lining. Sew seed beads along lower edge.

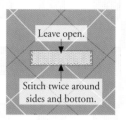

Leave open.

Stitch twice around sides and bottom.

7. Sew four large bugle beads at each intersection of one color of couched yarn. Sew four small bugle beads to remaining intersections.

8. Sew swan buttons in place.

CHRISTMAS CACTUS AND CURRANTS

The classic Christmas colors of red and green combine with lovely hand stitching for a look of traditional elegance. This hand appliquéd pillow will be a cherished gift for someone very special on your Christmas list.

Finished Size: 14" x 14"

FABRIC REQUIREMENTS

Fabric A (*pillow top, back, and backing*) - 1 yard medium gold

Fabric B (*cactus leaves and stems*) scraps of assorted green prints

Fabric C (*cactus flower and currants*) - scraps of assorted red prints

Fabric D (*dark currants*) - small scrap of black

Fabric E (*center and large currants*) - scrap of bright gold

Sharp lead pencil

Template plastic

Thread to match appliqué fabrics

Lightweight batting 18" square

Pillow form - 14" square

CUTTING

Refer to steps 1-3 of Hand Appliqué on page 138 to cut and prepare appliqués for stitching.

Fabric A (*medium gold*)
    Two 18" squares for pillow top and backing
    Two 9½" x 14½" pieces for pillow back

Fabric B (*green*)
    Four leaves
    Four stems

Fabric C (*red*)
    Eight flower petals
    Four flower buds
    Twelve currants

Fabric D (*black*) Twelve currants

Fabric E (*bright gold*)
    One flower center
    Four currants

MAKING THE PILLOW TOP

1. Fold 16" square of background fabric in half diagonally and then in half again and crease to mark center.
2. Position background square over design and use a sharp lead pencil to trace design onto right side of fabric. Trace inside the design lines to ensure that appliqués will cover traced lines completely. Rotate background square and repeat to trace entire design.

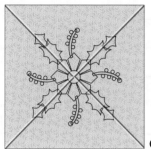

Creases

3. Position and sew appliqués to background, following steps 4-7 of Hand Appliqué on page 138. Press completed work as directed.
4. Place batting square on wrong side of backing square. Place appliquéd piece on top. Baste layers together and hand or machine quilt as desired.
5. Trim square to 14½", making sure design is centered.

ASSEMBLING THE PILLOW COVER

1. Turn under and press ⅜" at one long edge of each 9½" x 14½" piece of background fabric. Turn under again and edge stitch. Lap pieces with turned edges in center so pillow backing is 14½" square. Baste layers together.

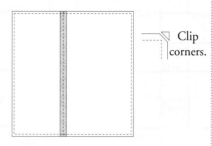

Clip corners.

2. With right sides together, stitch pillow top to pillow backing ¼" from raw edges. Clip corners and turn right side out.
3. Position pillow inside.

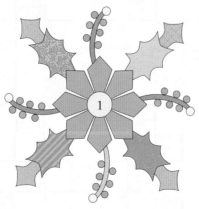

PILLOW APPLIQUÉ DESIGN

TO MAKE PERFECTLY ROUND CURRANTS

1. Draw a circle the finished size of the currant on a piece of stiff paper such as an index card. You will need twenty-four small and four large circles for this design. Cut out carefully.
2. Make ⅛"-long running stitches about ⅛" from the outer edge of each fabric circle. Begin and end this basting on the right side of the fabric circle.
3. Enclose paper circle inside a fabric circle by gently pulling on both ends of the basting thread and knot thread ends. Trim.
4. Press and position circle on appliqué fabric background. Sew in place.
5. To remove paper, turn work over and make a tiny slit in background fabric only. Carefully pull paper out with tweezers.

SOMETHING EXTRA

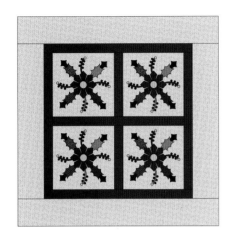

Use the Christmas Cactus and Currants design to create a treasured holiday wallhanging for your home. Appliqué the design to four 18" background squares. Trim to 14½" and make into a 4-block wall hanging with contrasting lattice strips around blocks. Add an outer border, then layer, quilt as desired, and bind the edges.

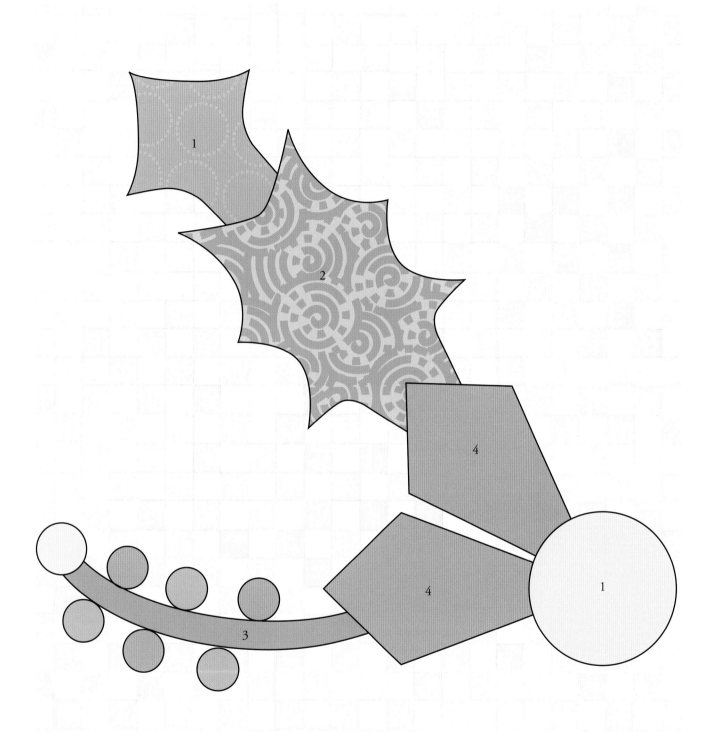

PILLOW APPLIQUÉ

EIGHT MAIDS~A~MILKING

EIGHTMAIDS A~MILKING

*On the eighth day of Christmas,
my true love sent to me,
Eight Maids-a-Milking ...*

A h ... to have the helping hands of eight maids during this magical, but hectic season. But don't despair ... just take time to relax and enjoy the enchantment of this special once-a-year time.

EIGHT QUICK AND EASY GIFTS

It happens every year. There are so many things to do ... and not enough time to do them. We can help! With these great ideas, you'll be able to create festive gifts with your own personal handmade touch ... and still have time left to spare!

SAND-PAINTING BROWNIES

Rich and chocolaty brownies are always a treat. This scrumptious and fun-to-make gift is great for your kids to put together while you stitch up the decorative lids. Perfect for a neighbor or a special teacher.

MATERIALS NEEDED

Apothecary jar - 4"-diameter, 7" tall

Ingredients in step 1 on page 89

One 4½" x 28" strip of red print (or 4½" x 2½ times jar circumference)

One 1¾" x 28" strip of green print (or 1¾" x 2½ times jar circumference)

One 10½" piece of ⅜"-wide elastic (or circumference of jar neck)

Decorative porcelain button

EIGHT MAIDS-A-MILKING

MAKING THE JAR GARTER

1. Turn under and press ¼" at each end of the red and green fabric strips. Turn again and stitch.
2. Fold 4" strip in half lengthwise with right sides together. Stitch ¼" from long raw edges. Turn right side out and press.
3. Fold 1¾" strip in half lengthwise with wrong sides together and stitch ¼" from long raw edges. Center seam on underside of stitched strip.
4. Center narrow strip on top of wide strip and edge stitch in place to make casing for elastic.

5. Thread elastic through casing, overlap ends, and stitch securely. Hide stitched end inside the garter.
6. Sew decorative button to center front. Slip garter over neck of jar of brownie mix. Attach recipe tag.

MAKING THE BROWNIE MIX

Yield: Seven cups of mix

1. Layer the following ingredients in the jar in order:
   ½ tsp. salt
   ½ cup, plus 2 T. flour
   ⅓ cup cocoa
   ½ cup flour
   ⅔ cup brown sugar
   ⅔ cup granulated sugar
   ⅓ cup chocolate chips
   ⅓ cup peanut butter chips
   ⅓ cup white chocolate chips
   ½ cup coarsely chopped pecans, or enough to fill jar

2. Write the following instructions for preparation and baking on a small tag:

Sand-Painting Brownie Mix

Preheat oven to 350° F.

Combine contents of jar with 1 tsp. vanilla, ⅔ cup salad oil, and 3 eggs. Mix well.

Bake in greased 9" x 9" pan for about 30 minutes. Allow to cool and cut into nine pieces.

HOT CHOCOLATE MIX

What goes perfectly with our irresistible brownies? Hot chocolate, of course! Add a jar of this delicious mix to a basket with a jar of Sand-Painting Brownie mix, and your mouth-watering gift is ready to deliver!

MATERIALS NEEDED

Decorative jars in assorted
  sizes
Hot Chocolate Mix
  (see recipe below)
Gift card

Scraps of holiday fabrics
Scrap of fusible web
  (*without paper backing*)
Grosgrain ribbon - ¾"-wide
Small bell

MAKING THE HOT CHOCOLATE MIX

1. Place the following ingredients in a large mixing bowl. Stir to mix thoroughly.
   15-ounce container of chocolate-flavored powdered drink mix (*3½ cups*)
   9.6-ounce box of nonfat dry milk powder
   ½ cup powdered coffee creamer*
   ½ cup powdered sugar
   Try a flavored version—peppermint or amaretto, for example.

2. Spoon mix into decorative jars and seal. Use a funnel to make it easier to get mix into jars with small openings.
3. Write the following directions on the gift card: Stir ¼ cup of mix into a 6-ounce cup full of hot water. Enjoy!

MAKING THE COVERS

1. Measure diameter of container top and add 4½".
2. Cut two fabric squares (matching or contrasting) that are at least ½" larger than this measurement. (For a 4"-diameter jar, cut two 9" squares). Draw a circle on wrong side of one square.
3. With the two squares right sides together, stitch on drawn line. Cut out ¼" beyond stitching. Make a small slit in one fabric layer in center of circle and turn cover right side out.
4. Tuck a small piece of fusible web into cover under slit. Bring cut edges together and fuse, following manufacturer's directions.
5. Place fabric cover over jar top and tie in place with a length of grosgrain ribbon. Tie a bow and embellish with small bell.

TIP

For a smoothly turned circle, use pinking shears to cut out the circles. It automatically notches the seam allowance, removing excess fabric.

EMBOSSED VELVET SCARF

*Truly an elegant gift …
this scarf of rich, embossed velvet is
sure to be treasured. It's so simple
to create you can do it in an evening!*

Finished Size: 8½" x 65"
(without fringe)

MATERIALS NEEDED

Velvet (*rayon or rayon-blend*)
⅝ yard
Silky polyester lining
⅝ yard

Rayon fringe - ½ yard of
4" long, (*try the fabric store
home dec department*)
**Decorative rubber stamp or
embroidered lace**

CUTTING

Velvet - two 9" x 42" strips
Lining - two 9" x 42" strips

EMBOSSING AND MAKING THE SCARF

1. Sew velvet strips right sides together to make one long strip. Trim to 65½", taking care to center seam line.
2. Emboss velvet, following embossing directions on page 47.
3. Baste lining to scarf with wrong sides together. Roll velvet edge under twice and hand slipstitch to lining only.
4. Hand or machine stitch fringe to each end, turning under raw edges at each end.

HATS! HATS! HATS!

A winter chapeau all decked out for the holidays – what fun to wear! Start with a purchased hat and add gorgeous ribbons and trims and bits of jewelry you've been saving. Use your imagination and create a fanciful hat for each of your special friends to wear to a Christmas tea.

MATERIALS NEEDED

Felt or faux fur hats
Assorted ribbons and trims
Decorative buttons and "junk" jewelry

Feathers
Glitter netting
Anything else that strikes your fancy!

TRIMMING THE HATS

Hand sew ribbon trims or glitter netting to the brim or crown. Add a bow of the same trim. Embellish with your choice of pieces of jewelry or decorative buttons and/or feathers.

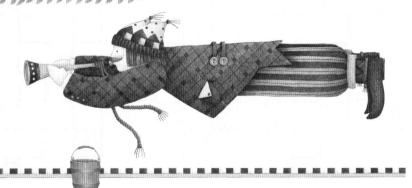

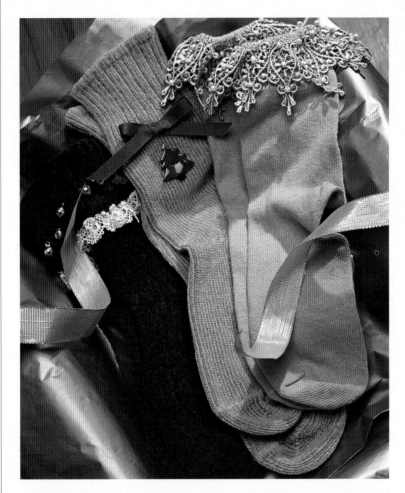

TW!NKLE T!ES

Christmas stockings never
looked so stunning …
and it couldn't be easier!
A few stitches and some
clever embellishments
add up to wearing
fun for the holidays.

MATERIALS NEEDED

Purchased socks
Lace
Beads

Jingle bells
Buttons
Ribbon

EMBELLISHING IDEAS

Turn cuff down and hand sew narrow cotton lace edging to edge of ribbing, stretching out the ribbing as you stitch. When you let go, the lace ruffles automatically. Add small jingle bells.

Add wide lace trim to top edge of cotton socks and embellish with beads.

Sew buttons and bows to each sock in pairs.

SCENTED PINECONES

For a cozy, country touch, place a basket of scented pinecones on your hearth to scent the room – or toss them into the fire and enjoy the warm fragrance. Make enough for all your friends too.

MATERIALS NEEDED

One dozen large Ponderosa pinecones
Basket
Wide beaded ribbon
  3 yards
Refresher or essential oil
  of your choice
  (*0.5-fluid ounce bottle will scent over 100 pinecones*)

ASSEMBLY

1. Allow pinecones to dry thoroughly.
2. Hold cones over a plastic bag or layers of newspaper and apply one drop of oil to each. The fragrance will not be strong but may intensify over time.
3. Arrange cones in basket and add a decorative ribbon bow.

CHARMED TREE

This charming little tree will add a touch of holiday spirit to any spot. Decorated with charms, buttons, and beads, it sits in a tiny painted terra cotta pot.

Finished Size: 5" x 8" (approximate)

MATERIALS NEEDED

Green prints, assorted
    Fifty 2" squares
Polyester fiberfill
Pewter buttons and charms
    Assorted, small
Glass beads - Small, red
Satin Ribbon - ⅛"-wide,
    burgundy
Dowel - 7½" piece of
    ½"-diameter, painted brown

Terra cotta pot - 1½"-tall,
    1¼" top diameter
Acrylic paint - black, country red,
    antique white, green, gold
Small paintbrushes
Spray matte varnish
Crackling medium
Plaster of Paris
Craft glue
Sphagnum Moss

MAKING THE TREE

1. Arrange fifty squares for two five-patch blocks. Sew together in rows and press seams in opposite directions row to row. Sew rows together for each block. Press seams in one direction.
2. Make a paper tracing or plastic template of the tree pattern on page 98.
3. Place blocks right sides together, position and trace tree pattern onto patchwork block. Stitch on drawn lines, leaving opening for turning at bottom edge. Cut out ¼" from stitching line. Trim across points and clip corners, but not through stitching.
4. Turn tree right side out and stuff lightly, using a chopstick or small dowel to poke bits of fiberfill into points of tree.
5. Embellish tree with buttons, charms, beads, and small bows.

PAINTING THE POT

1. Refer to Painting Techniques on page 139 to paint the pot.
2. After preparing pot, paint interior and lower pot black. Apply crackling medium, followed by country red paint.
3. Paint pot rim antique white. Using small clear ruler and soft-lead pencil, mark a narrow checkerboard pattern along lower edge of rim. Paint every other square black.
4. Using a small liner brush, paint a gold vine above the checkerboard, adding green leaves and red dots for berries.
5. Spray with matte varnish, apply antiquing medium, then a final coat of matte varnish.

ASSEMBLING THE TREE

1. Slightly sharpen one end of 7½" length of brown dowel.
2. Prepare enough plaster of Paris to fill pot ¾ full. Put flat end of dowel in center of pot and surround with plaster. Allow to dry.
3. Poke pointed end of dowel into center of tree. Add a small amount of craft glue under the opening edges and "pinch" to the dowel.
4. Glue sphagnum moss on top of dried plaster.

TOPIARY PINCUSHIONS

Sitting together in the sewing room, these fanciful little trees add a touch of fun décor, besides being a handy place to keep quilting pins. For even more fun, make more than two!

MATERIALS NEEDED
(BOTH TREES)

Green holiday fabric - Two 7" x 12" pieces
Polyester fiberfill
Terra cotta pots with bases - 3" tall, 3½" diameter for heart; 2" tall, 2½" diameter for tree
Acrylic paints - ivory, red, dark green, gold, black
Spray matte varnish

Crackling medium
Assorted small paintbrushes
Toothbrush
Small sponge
Craft glue
Bead trim
Dowel - 18"-long piece of ¼"-diameter, stained brown
Plaster of Paris
Sphagnum moss

PAINTING THE POTS

1. Refer to Painting Techniques on page 139 to prepare and paint the pots and pot bases.
2. After preparing the pots, paint as directed in the diagram of each pot, allowing to dry thoroughly after each step.

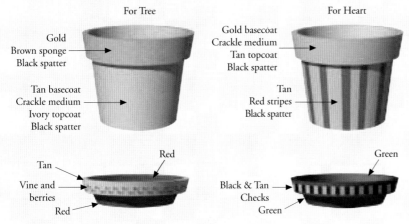

For Tree

Gold
Brown sponge
Black spatter

Tan basecoat
Crackle medium
Ivory topcoat
Black spatter

For Heart

Gold basecoat
Crackle medium
Tan topcoat
Black spatter

Tan
Red stripes
Black spatter

Tan
Vine and berries
Red

Red

Green

Black & Tan Checks
Green

3. Glue pot bottom to base.
4. Glue bead trim around upper edge of pot.

CREATE A CARD

For a Christmas greeting with your own personal touch, create festive fabric trees on your cards. Stitch together lots of scrappy five-patch blocks in Christmas colors and cut trees from each of them using the tree pattern. With gold metallic thread zigzag trees and grosgrain ribbon "trunks" to card stock. Embellish with bows and beads glued in place. Glue to a larger piece of card stock in a contrasting color and cut with decorative edges. Write your holiday greeting on the back and send in a pretty envelope.

MAKING THE HEART AND TREE

1. Using the patterns on pages 98-99, cut two hearts from one piece of green fabric. Cut one circle and one tree from remaining piece of green fabric.
2. With hearts right sides together, stitch ¼" from raw edges, leaving opening at point for dowel and an opening on one side for turning. Clip inner point at top of heart and notch out excess fabric on curves.

Clip.

Backstitch.

Turn through opening.

Open for dowel

3. Turn heart right side out and stuff firmly. Hand sew opening closed on side.
4. Fold tree in half with right sides together and stitch ¼" from raw edges, leaving an opening for turning and stuffing.

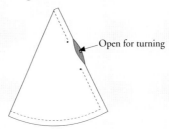

Open for turning

5. On circle, machine stitch a ⅜"-diameter circle in center. Mark an **X** in center and clip to stitching.

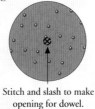

Stitch and slash to make opening for dowel.

6. Sew circle to bottom edge of tree. Turn tree right side out and stuff firmly.

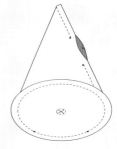

7. Cut two 8" lengths of dowel and sharpen one end of each. Insert pointed end in opening at bottom of heart and in opening in bottom of tree. Glue in place.
8. Prepare enough plaster of Paris to fill each pot ¾ full. Put flat end of each dowel in center of its painted pot and surround with plaster. Allow to dry.
9. Glue sphagnum moss on top of plaster.

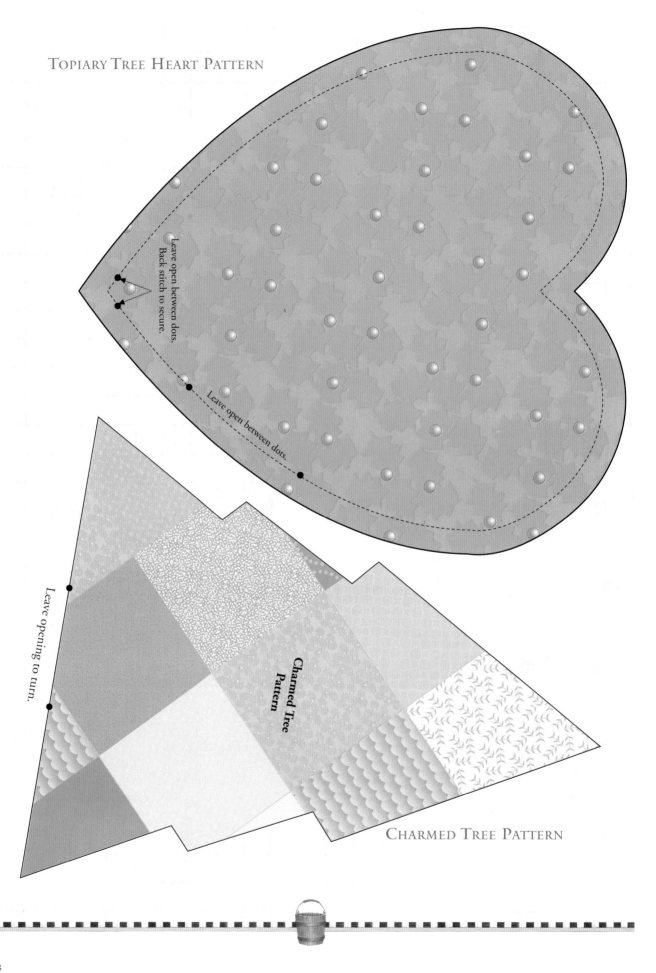

TOPIARY TREE HEART PATTERN

Leave open between dots.
Back stitch to secure.

Leave open between dots.

Leave opening to turn.

Charmed Tree
Pattern

CHARMED TREE PATTERN

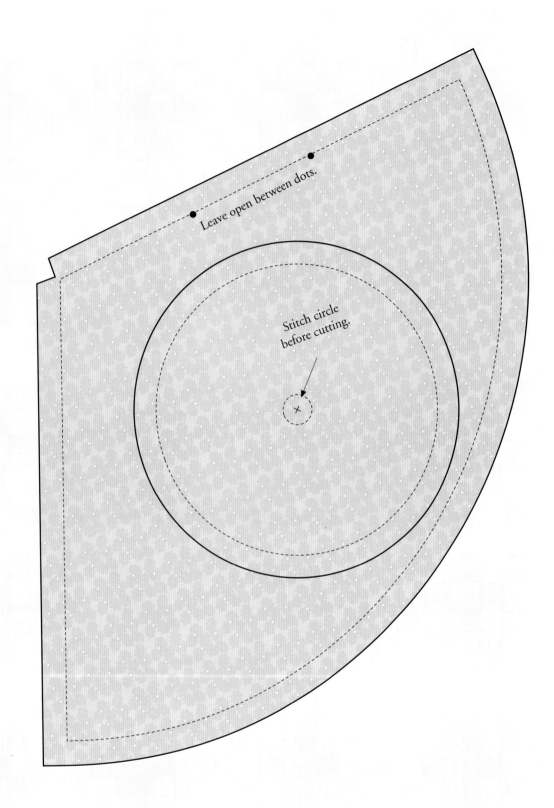

Leave open between dots.

Stitch circle
before cutting.

TOPIARY TREE PINCUSHION PATTERN

NINE LADIES DANCING

NINE LADIES
DANCING

On the ninth day of Christmas,
my true love sent to me,
Nine Ladies Dancing ...

Nine ladies dancing ...Where there's dancing, there's usually celebrating! Since the Twelve Days of Christmas season is all about celebrating, add a little dancing to your holiday festivities.

Lady's Lounging Robe and Slippers

After an exciting evening of wonderful dancing … or maybe just a frantic day of holiday shopping … slip into this cozy robe and slippers for relaxing time in front of the fire. Just the right attire for Christmas morning too!

MATERIALS NEEDED

SLIPPERS

White fleece slippers
One pair
Felted wool - Two 4" squares
of dark green
Fusible web - 4" square
Embroidery floss - dark green
Decorative cord - 1¼ yards
Jingle bells - Two large

ROBE

Purchased fleece robe
red with shawl collar
and patch pockets
Felted wool or just felt
One 6" square of green
Embroidery floss - dark green
Decorative cord - 2-3 yards
Jingle bells - Twelve small

NINE LADIES DANCING

EMBELLISHING THE SLIPPERS

1. Fuse felt squares together with layer of fusible web in between, following manufacturer's directions.

2. Using large holly leaf pattern, trace and cut four leaves from felt layers.

3. Blanket stitch over raw edges of each holly leaf. Use stem stitch to embroider veins. Refer to Embroidery Stitch Guide on page 138.

4. Tack leaves together in pairs.

5. Cut decorative cord in half and tie a bow in center of each. Whipstitch cord to slipper. Add holly leaves and a gold jingle bell.

EMBELLISHING THE ROBE

1. Using the small holly leaf pattern, trace around and cut ten from green felted wool. Blanket stitch over all raw edges and use stem stitch to embroider veins on leaves. (Make two or three additional holly leaves if you want them to extend all the way around the collar).

2. Whipstitch decorative cord to collar in a meandering, vine-like pattern. Arrange three holly leaves on each collar front and tack in place. Add three jingle bells.

3. Whipstitch cord to each patch pocket and embellish each with two holly leaves and a cluster of three jingle bells.

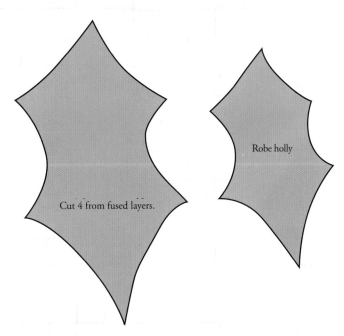

Robe holly

Cut 4 from fused layers.

HOLLY PATTERN FOR ROBE AND SLIPPERS

TEN LORDS~A~LEAPING

TEN LORDS~A~LEAPING

On the tenth day of Christmas,
my true love sent to me,
Ten Lords-a-Leaping ...

Feasting on tasty delicacies is a favorite part of the holiday season. Nothing creates a festive occasion like sharing a delicious meal, good conversation, and joyous laughter around the table.

LORD OF THE MANOR

LORD OF THE MANOR APRON AND CHEF'S HAT

*Let the Lord of the Manor
take over chef duties for
Christmas brunch.
Coax him into the kitchen
with this dapper chef's hat
and apron and let him
do the cooking while you
set a festive table*

FABRIC REQUIREMENTS

CHEF'S APRON

Canvas chef's apron

Fabric A (*red band*)
3" x 15" strip

Fabric B (*checkerboard band*)
1⅞" x 15" strip

Fabric C (*wreath*)
One 12½" square

Assorted fabric scraps in desired colors (*refer to photo for ideas*)

Lightweight fusible web
½ yard

Thread to match appliqué fabrics

Beads or doll buttons
Three small

Embroidery floss - black

Optional - 4" toy spatula and fork

CHEF'S HAT

Fabric A (*crown*) - ⅛ yard black and white check print

Fabric B (*band*) - ⅛ yard dark red

Interfacing - One 4" x 24½" strip medium-weight fusible

Elastic - 1"-wide, 5"-long

TEN LORDS ~A~ LEAPING

EMBELLISHING THE APRON

1. Turn under and press ¼" at each long edge of Fabric A and B strips. Center Fabric B strip on Fabric Strip A and edge stitch in place.

2. Measure top edge of apron and add ¾". Trim strip from step 1 to this measurement. Pin to apron with top edges even and turn under short ends even with apron edge. Pin. Edge stitch in place.

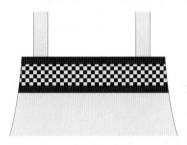

3. Referring to Quick-Fuse Appliqué on page 139, apply fusible web to wrong side of Fabric C (*wreath*) 12" square and to wrong side of selected appliqué fabrics.

4. Refer to leaping lord appliqué pattern on page 114 and trace each shape onto desired fabrics.

5. Cut out shapes and fuse to apron. *If you are using toy utensils instead of utensil appliqués, do not fuse the hands to apron.* Finish fused edges with machine satin stitch or decorative stitching. Blanket stitch around each hand and attach to cuffs. Then attach hands to utensils and background with a few hand stitches.

6. Embroider a French knot for lord's eye and add beads or buttons to front edge of vest.

7. Add a pocket watch charm to lord's vest if you wish.

CHEF'S HAT
CUTTING

Fabric A - One 26½"-diameter circle
Fabric B - One 4¼" x 25" strip

MAKING THE HAT

1. Machine baste ¼" from outside edge of Fabric A crown. Gather.

2. Following manufacturer's directions, fuse interfacing to wrong side of Fabric B hatband. (Interfacing is slightly smaller than band.)

3. Fold hatband in half lengthwise with wrong sides together, mark embroidery placement,* and center it in band strip. Unfold strip and embroider.

* We used the Bernina embroidery machine and chose all capital letters in the medium size.

4. With right sides of band together, stitch ¼" from short end, leaving a 1½" opening ½" above bottom edge as shown in diagram.

5. Turn under and press ¼" along top edge of band. Pin the right side of bottom edge of band to wrong side of Fabric A crown, adjusting gathers to fit. Stitch.

6. Turn folded edge of band to inside and pin in place along stitching line. Topstitch through all layers.

7. If desired insert a 5" length of 1"-wide elastic into 1½" opening on band. Stitch one end to band, adjust elastic to fit, and stitch other end in place.

CHRISTMAS BRUNCH TABLE RUNNER

While your Lord of the Manor is whipping up the family's Christmas brunch, you can set the holiday table accented with this festive table runner. Quick and easy to make, you will enjoy using it the rest of the year too.

Finished Size: 16½" x 50½"

FABRIC REQUIREMENTS

Fabric A (*dark red*) - ½ yard
Fabric B (*bright gold*) - ⅓ yard
Fabric C (*dark green*) - ¼ yard
Fabric D (*light tan print #1*) ¼ yard
Fabric E (*light tan print #2*) ⅙ yard

Fabric F (*medium tan print #1*) - ⅙ yard
Fabric G (*medium tan print #2*) - ⅛ yard
Binding (*dark red*) ⅜ yard
Batting - 1 yard
Backing - 1⅛ yard

CUTTING THE STRIPS AND PIECES

Read first paragraph of Cutting the Strips and Pieces on page 14.

Fabric A (*dark red*) -
One 8¾" x 42" strip, cut into
- One 8¾" square
- Two 8½" x 13½" pieces

One 6" x 42" strip, cut into
- Two 6" squares

Fabric B (*bright gold*)
Three 3¼" x 42" strips, cut into
- Two 3¼" x 14¼" strips
- Two 3¼" x 8¾" strips
- Eight 3¼" x 6" pieces

Fabric C (*dark green*)
One 2½" x 42" strip, cut into
- Four 2½" x 8½" strips

One 3¼" x 42" strip, cut into
- Eight 3¼" squares

Fabric D (*light tan print #1*)
Three 2½" x 42" strips

Fabric E (*light tan print #2*)
Two 2½" x 42" strips

Fabric F (*dark tan print #1*)
Two 2½" x 42" strips

Fabric G (*dark tan print #2*)
One 2½" x 42" strip

Backing
Two 20" x 42" strips cut into
- One 20" x 40¼" strip
- One 20" x 14¼" strip

Binding - Four - 2¾" x 42" strips

MAKING THE BLOCKS

1. Sew a 3¼" Fabric C square to opposite ends of each of four 3¼" x 6" Fabric B strips. Press toward Fabric B. Make Four.
2. Sew remaining 3¼" x 6" Fabric B strips to opposite edges of each 6" Fabric A square. Press seams toward Fabric B.
3. Arrange units from steps 1 and 2 to make two nine-patch blocks. Sew pieces together and press seams toward Fabric B.

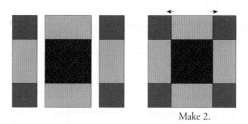

Make 2.

4. Sew tan strips together in pairs as shown in diagram.

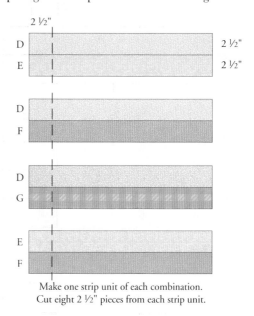

Make one strip unit of each combination.
Cut eight 2 ½" pieces from each strip unit.

5. Cut eight 2½"-wide pieces from each strip unit from step 4. Arrange and sew units into rows. Press.

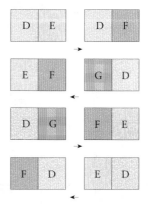

6. Arrange rows from step 5 as shown in diagram to make four blocks. Sew rows together and press. Block measures 8½" x 8½".

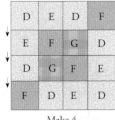

D	E	D	F
E	F	G	D
D	G	F	E
F	D	E	D

Make 4.

7. Cut each block from step 6 in half diagonally.

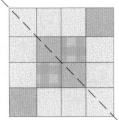

Cut in half diagonally.

8. Sew four triangles from step 7 to each nine-patch block. Press seams toward blocks.

9. Sew a 3¼" x 8¾" Fabric B strip to opposite edges of 8¾" Fabric A square. Press.

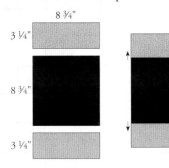

8 ¾"

3 ¼"

8 ¾"

3 ¼"

10. Sew a 3¼" x 14¼ Fabric B strip to remaining edges of Fabric A square. Press.

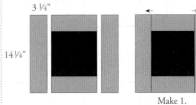

3 ¼"

14¼"

Make 1.

11. Sew a 2½" x 8½" Fabric C strip to the short edges of each 8½" x 13½" Fabric A piece. Press seam toward Fabric C. Make two.

12. From each unit from step 11, cut two triangles as shown in diagram. Diagonal cut will measure 12".

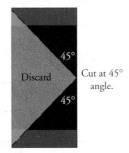

Discard

45°

45°

Cut at 45° angle.

13. Place triangle on top of square from step 10 allowing ¼" of triangle point to extend as shown. Sew and press. Repeat for other sides positioning as shown. Trim gold strips even with triangle edges.

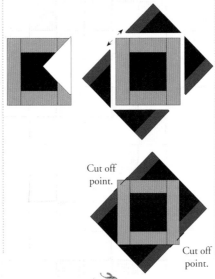

Cut off point.

Cut off point.

14. Sew nine-patch blocks to center block. Press seams toward center block.

LAYERING AND FINISHING

1. With right sides together, stitch backing pieces together to make a strip 20" x 54" long.

2. Arrange and baste backing, batting, and runner together, referring to Layering the Quilt on page 138.

3. Machine or hand quilt as desired. Trim backing and batting even with quilt top edges.

4. Cut two binding strips in half. Sew one strip to each remaining long strip.

5. Bind quilt, referring to Binding the Quilt on page 139.

BRUNCH CENTERPIECE

Add the perfect touch of country elegance to your Christmas brunch with this charming live tree centerpiece adorned with dried fruit garlands. Make it a family affair with the kids stringing the dried apples, oranges, pears, and cranberries.

MATERIALS NEEDED

Ceramic pot with matte finish, approximately 8" tall

Plywood - 12" square piece, ¼" thick for birds or use purchased wooden birds, approximately 2¼" x 5¼"

Acrylic craft paints - country red, dark green, antique gold, gray, charcoal, ivory, tan, brown, black

Rusted craft tin - one sheet

Spray matte varnish

Antiquing medium

Clear ruler

White chalk pencil

Soft-lead pencil

Assorted paintbrushes

Toothpick

Wood stain - light brown

Old toothbrush

Old scissors

Epoxy Glue

Dried apples, oranges, pears, cranberries

Bay leaves

Nylon fish line - clear, approximately 5 yards

Live or artificial tree - approximately 28" tall

Florist's foam - (*optional*)

Sphagnum moss

PAINTING THE POT

1. Read through Painting Techniques on page 139 and prepare pot as directed.
2. Study the decorative areas of your pot and decide on your painting scheme.
3. For checkerboard area, paint desired area gray and use a white chalk pencil to draw a grid of squares. Paint every other square charcoal.
4. To add vine detail, use a small liner brush and dip toothpick in red paint to add berries.
5. When painting is complete, add a coat of spray varnish and allow to dry.
6. Antique painted pot with antiquing medium, following manufacturer's directions.
7. Finish with one more coat of spray varnish.

PAINTING THE BIRDS

1. Transfer bird patterns to plywood. Cut out and sand. Apply ivory base coat to birds, painting one that faces left and one that faces right. Allow to dry.
2. Referring to bird pattern on page 113 and using clear ruler and soft-lead pencil, draw ¼" checkerboard pattern on bird body, polka dots on head, and tail feather details. Paint tan dots in head and every other square and tail feather tan. Add brown feather details using a small liner brush. Paint beak antique gold and add a narrow stripe of gold at neck and tail.
3. Spatter with brown paint (see page 139) and add a black dot for the eye.
4. Add a coat of spray matte varnish, then apply antiquing medium following manufacturer's directions. Add one more coat of spray varnish (or marine varnish for outdoor use).

6. Cut two wings from rusted tin. Bend each wing slightly for dimension, then use epoxy glue to attach wings to birds.

ASSEMBLING THE CENTERPIECE

1. Purchase dried fruit or slice and dry fresh fruit in a food dehydrator.
2. Using a large-eyed needle, string dried oranges, cranberries, and bay leaves on clear nylon fish line. Pierce dried pears, add a loop of fish line and hang from garland. You will need approximately 90" of finished garland, depending on size of tree.

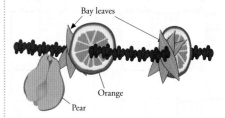

Bay leaves

Orange

Pear

3. Place tree in pot, using blocks of florist's foam to hold trunk firmly in place if necessary. Cover top of foam or root ball of live tree with sphagnum moss.
4. Wrap fruit garland around tree.
5. Add birds to treetop, attaching loosely with wire.

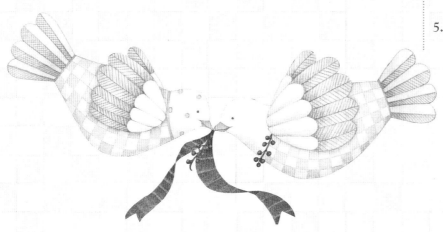

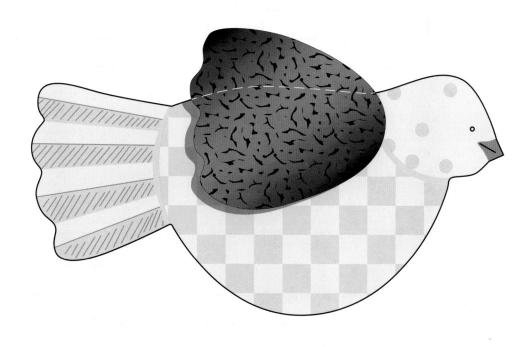

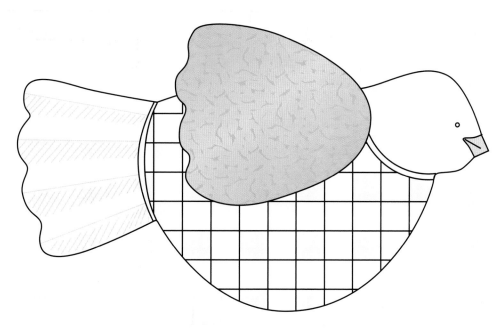

BRUNCH CENTERPIECE BIRD PATTERN

LORD OF THE MANOR APRON TEMPLATE
Enlarge template to 165%
Appliqué is reversed for use with Quick-Fuse Appliqué
(Project instructions page 106)

CHRISTMAS BRUNCH

*It's even more fun when the whole family helps with the festivities.
How about a new holiday tradition ... the Lord of the Manor
is in charge of Christmas Brunch! It's easy ... we've created
a delicious menu and the recipes are easy to follow.*

TRIPLE BERRY SAUCE

MIMOSAS WITH A TWIST

WHOLE-WHEAT BANANA WAFFLES

CRANBERRY ORANGE SAUCE

CHRISTMAS BREAKFAST SAUSAGE

MORNING GLORY MUFFINS

MIMOSAS WITH A TWIST

SERVES 12

1 BOTTLE CHAMPAGNE
1 (64-OUNCE) BOTTLE
  CRANBERRY JUICE
1 (64-OUNCE) CARTON
  ORANGE JUICE
1 (64-OUNCE) CARTON
  PINK GRAPEFRUIT JUICE

METHOD: *Mix all ingredients together in large punch bowl. Serve over ice and garnish with fruit skewers.*

CRANBERRY ORANGE SAUCE

SERVES 12

2 ORANGES
1 SMALL BAG
  CRANBERRIES
½ CUP SUGAR
½ CUP ORANGE JUICE
WATER, AS NEEDED

METHOD: *Peel and section the oranges and cut sections into bite-size pieces and set aside. Place cranberries, sugar, and orange juice in a small saucepan. Bring to a boil, reduce heat, and simmer until the cranberries are soft and have reached a sauce-like consistency. Add water if too thick. Just before serving, add orange pieces. Serve hot or cold.*

WHOLE WHEAT BANANA WAFFLES

SERVES 12

¼ CUP BUTTER
1 CUP MILK
3 EGGS
1 TABLESPOON HONEY
2 CUPS WHOLE WHEAT FLOUR
½ TEASPOON SALT
2 TEASPOONS BAKING
  POWDER
1-2 BANANAS, MASHED

METHOD: *Melt the butter, let cool slightly. In a 2-cup glass measuring cup, measure out milk. Add eggs, honey, and cooled butter. Mix well. Sift flour, salt, and baking powder together into a bowl and form a well. Pour the egg mixture into the well. Mix gently. Fold in the mashed banana. Bake in waffle iron.*

TRIPLE BERRY SAUCE

SERVES 12

½ CUP FROZEN
  BLUEBERRIES
½ CUP FROZEN
  BLACKBERRIES OR RASP-
  BERRIES
½ CUP FROZEN
  STRAWBERRIES
¾ CUP SUGAR
½ CUP WATER

METHOD: *Place frozen fruit, sugar, and water in saucepan. Bring to a boil on high. Reduce heat to low and simmer until thick (about 20 minutes).*

MORNING GLORY MUFFINS

SERVES 12

½ CUP BROWN SUGAR

1½ CUPS FLOUR

1½ TEASPOONS CINNA-
MON

½ TEASPOON SALT

1 TEASPOON BAKING SODA

¼ CUP SHREDDED
COCONUT, OPTIONAL

¼ CUP WALNUTS,
COARSELY CHOPPED

½ CUP DRIED
CRANBERRIES

1 APPLE, GRATED

2 CARROTS, PEELED
AND GRATED

1 (8-OUNCE) CAN
CRUSHED PINEAPPLE,
WELL-DRAINED

2 EGGS

¼ CUP VEGETABLE OIL

1 STICK BUTTER, MELTED

2 TEASPOONS LEMON
JUICE

½ TEASPOON VANILLA

METHOD: *Pre-heat oven to 350° F. Line muffin tins with cupcake liners. Mix brown sugar, flour, cinnamon, salt, and baking soda in a large bowl. Add the coconut, walnuts, dried cranberries, grated apple, grated carrot, and pineapple in a bowl and mix until well incorporated. In a separate bowl, mix together eggs, oil, butter, lemon juice, and vanilla. Form a well in the dry ingredients, and add the liquid ingredients. The secret to light muffins is not to over-mix the ingredients, just mix until all of the flour is incorporated.*

Bake for 35 minutes, or until golden and a toothpick inserted into the middle of muffin comes out clean. The muffins should have a nice dome shape.

CHRISTMAS BREAKFAST SAUSAGE

SERVES 12

½ SMALL ONION

1 SHALLOT

2 CLOVES GARLIC

1 LB. PORK LOIN

½ CAN BEER

2 TABLESPOONS DRIED
CRANBERRIES

½ TEASPOON SALT

½ TEASPOON ALLSPICE

1 TABLESPOON CORN
SYRUP

OIL FOR SAUTÉ

METHOD: *Mince the onion, shallot, garlic, and pork loin. Sauté the onion, shallot, and garlic in a little oil. Add half the beer and the cranberries, let cook down until little of the liquid remains. Let the mixture cool completely. Mix together the cold minced pork loin, spices, onion mixture, the rest of the beer, and corn syrup. Make sure the mixture stays very cold. Form into patties and cook in a skillet until cooked through-out. The sausage can be made in advance and frozen into a log, thawed, and cut into patties when ready to cook.*

ELEVEN PIPERS PIPING

ELEVEN PIPERS PIPING

*On the eleventh day of Christmas,
my true love sent to me,
Eleven Pipers Piping …*

*Ringing of bells, singing of carols,
happy voices raised in laughter ... these are
just a few of the musical sounds that announce
the arrival of this most joyous of seasons.*

WREATH DOOR BANNER

Three is always better than one! Especially when it comes to holiday surprises. This three-wreath banner will be a charming change from the traditional wreath on your front door.

Finished Size: 19" x 47"
(without fringe)
Finished block size: 12" square

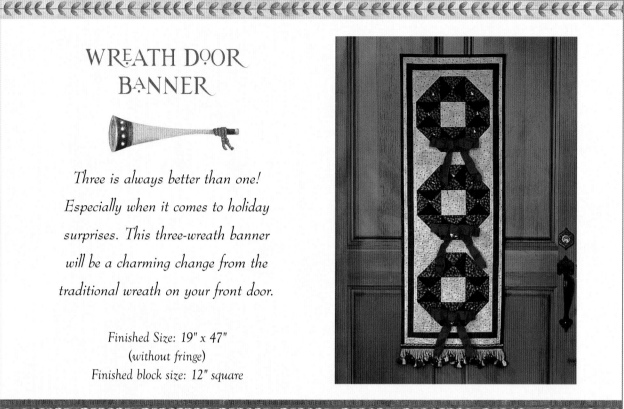

FABRIC REQUIREMENTS

Fabric A (*medium green*)
⅝ yard

Fabric B (*dark green*)
⅜ yard

Fabric C (*tan background and borders*) - ⅔ yard

Fabric D (*red accent border*)
⅙ yard

Binding - ⅓ yard

Backing - 1 yard

Batting - 21" x 51"

Ribbon - 6 yards of 1½"-wide, wire-edged

Ribbon - ¾ yard of narrow satin

Jingle bells - Nine (½" diameter)

Buttons - Twenty-one, gold (¾" diameter)

Fringe trim - ⅝ yard

ELEVEN PIPERS PIPING

CUTTING THE STRIPS AND PIECES

Read first paragraph of Cutting the Strips and Pieces on page 14.

Fabric A (*wreath*)

Two 4½" x 42" strips, cut into
- Twelve 4½" squares

Two 5¼" x 42" strips, cut into
- Twelve 5¼" squares

Fabric B (*wreath*)

Two 5¼" x 42" strips, cut into
- Twelve 5¼" squares

Fabric C (*background and borders*)

Two 4½" x 42" strips, cut into
- Fifteen 4½" squares

One 2½" x 42" strip, cut into
- Two 2½" x 12½" pieces

Two 1½" x 42" strips, cut into
- Two 1½" x 12½" pieces
- Two 1½" x 15½" pieces

Five 1" x 42" strips

Fabric D (*accent border*)

Three 1½" x 42" strips

Backing - One 24" x 42" pieces

One 9½" x 24" piece

Binding - Three 2¾" x 42" strips

MAKING THE BLOCKS

1. With right sides together and following directions for Quick Corner Triangles on page 138, stitch each of twelve 4½" Fabric A squares to a 4½" Fabric C square. Press.

4 ½"

4 ½"

A 4 ½" square
C 4 ½" square

Make 12.

2. Stitch each 5¼" Fabric A square to a 5¼" Fabric B square, following directions for quick corner triangles. Make twelve.

3. Cut each square from step 2 in half diagonally, cutting across the center seam.

Cut.

Make 12.

4. Arrange triangles from step 3 in pairs to create twelve squares. Sew together and press. Trim to 4½" x 4½".

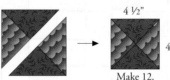

4 ½"

4 ½"

Make 12.

5. Arrange squares from steps 1 and 4 and 4½" Fabric C squares in rows to make three wreath blocks. Sew pieces together in rows. Press.

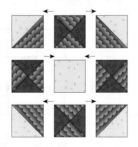

6. Sew rows together. Press.

7. Sew a 2½" x 12½" Fabric C strip to bottom edge of two blocks.

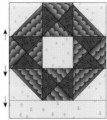

Make 2.

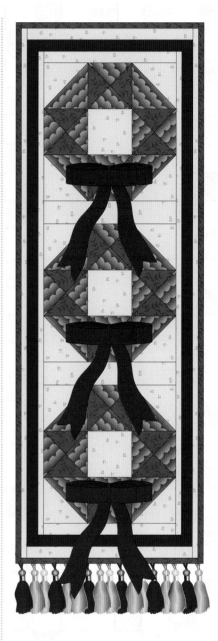

ASSEMBLY

1. Arrange and sew completed blocks together. Sew a 1½" x 12" Fabric C sashing strip to the top and bottom. Press.

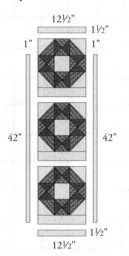

2. *Sew three 1" x 42" Fabric C strips together. Cut two strips, each 42½" long and set remainder aside for step 6. Sew to sides of banner. Press seam toward strip.

   Before sewing three strips together, check actual length of strips. If they are 42½" or longer, there is no need to sew three strips together.

3. Cut two 1½" x 13½" strips from a 1½" x 42" Fabric D strip. Sew to top and bottom edges of quilt. Press seam toward Fabric D strip.

4. Sew remainder of 1½" Fabric D strip to two remaining 1½"-wide Fabric D strips. Cut two 1½" x 44½" strips from long strip and sew to each side of quilt top.

5. Sew 1½" x 15½" Fabric C strips to top and bottom edge of quilt top. Press toward Fabric C strips.

6. Sew remainder of strip from step 2 to remaining 1" x 42" Fabric C strips. Cut two 1" x 46½" strips from long strip and sew to long edges of quilt top. Press toward Fabric C strips.

LAYERING AND FINISHING

1. Sew backing pieces together to make one long strip. Arrange and baste backing, batting, and top together, referring to Layering the Quilt on page 138.

2. Machine or hand quilt as desired. Trim backing and batting.

3. Cut two 19½"-long pieces from one binding strip. Sew to top and bottom edges of banner. Sew remaining binding strips together. Cut long strip into two pieces of equal length for sides of banner. Add binding, referring to Binding the Quilt on page 139.

4. Sew fringe to bottom edge of banner, turning raw edges under at sides of quilt.

5. Sew seven gold buttons to each wreath.

6. Cut wire-edge ribbon into three lengths. Make a bow from each by making three progressively smaller stacked loops. Pinch together in center and tie with short piece of narrow satin ribbon. Cut ribbon ends in an inward V. Tack bow to bottom of each wreath and embellish each with three jingle bells.

Narrow satin ribbon

MERRY CHRISTMAS TREE

During the Twelve Days of Christmas
you just can't have too many Christmas trees!
How about adding one to your front porch too.
Complete with its own charmingly painted pot,
you'll find elegant golden pears and birds
nestled in the branches of this festive tree.

MATERIALS NEEDED

Large flowerpot
Wooden bird & pear ornaments
 - cut from ¼" plywood
Rusted craft tin
 one thin sheet
Acrylic craft paints
 light antique gold, dark
 antique gold, dark brown,
 ivory, antique red, tan,
 black, medium gray
Assorted paint brushes

Clear ruler
Soft-lead pencil
Gesso
Toothbrush
Epoxy glue
Spray matte varnish
Marine varnish
Antiquing medium
Small hand drill
Sphagnum moss
⅛" wooden dowel

PAINTING THE POT

1. Read through Painting Directions on page 139 and prepare pot with a coat of gesso.

2. Decide on a painting plan for your pot, depending on its shape and design.

3. Complete painting as desired, allow to dry thoroughly, and add a coat of matte spray varnish.

4. Antique finished pot with antiquing medium, following manufacturer's directions.

5. Finish with two coats of marine varnish to make it weather-resistant for outdoor use.

6. Add a live tree to the pot with sphagnum moss around base.

PAINTING THE PARTRIDGE

1. Follow directions on page 112 for painting birds.
2. To paint partridge, refer to diagram and draw design lines on wooden partridge. Paint as shown in the diagram, using ivory for face, red in area around face, and black for top of head.

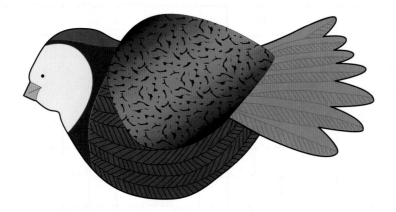

3. Paint underbelly medium gray and use a liner brush to add crosshatched feather details.
4. Paint tail feathers tan and add details in brown, using liner brush.
5. Paint beak gold and add black dot for eye.
6. Apply antiquing medium, following manufacturer's directions.
7. Finish with a coat of varnish.
8. Add 6"-long fish line loops to birds for hanging.
9. Add wings to partridge as directed for birds on page 112.
10. Hang ornaments on tree.

PAINTING THE PEARS

1. Drill small hole in top of each pear. Put a drop of glue in each hole and insert a small wooden dowel into hole for stem. Apply two coats of light antique gold, allowing to dry between coats.
2. Referring to patterns, draw designs on pears with soft-lead pencil.

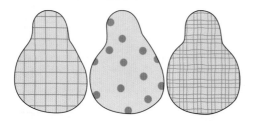

3. Paint designs with dark antique gold. Allow to dry. Paint stem dark brown.
4. Referring to Painting Techniques on page 139, spatter pears with dark brown paint.
5. Add a coat of spray matte varnish.
6. Apply antiquing medium following manufacturer's directions.
7. Finish with another coat of varnish.
8. Cut a rusted tin leaf for each pear, using template.
9. Cut a piece of rusted wire for each pear and wrap around pencil to curl. Slip off pencil. Pierce one end of leaf and slip a 6" piece of fish line and one end of curled wire through hole. Tie fish line ends together in overhand knot. Drill a small hole in pear and slip wire through. Wrap wire around itself to secure.

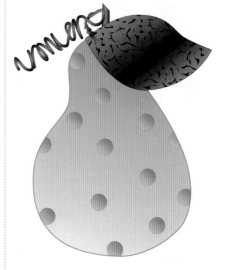

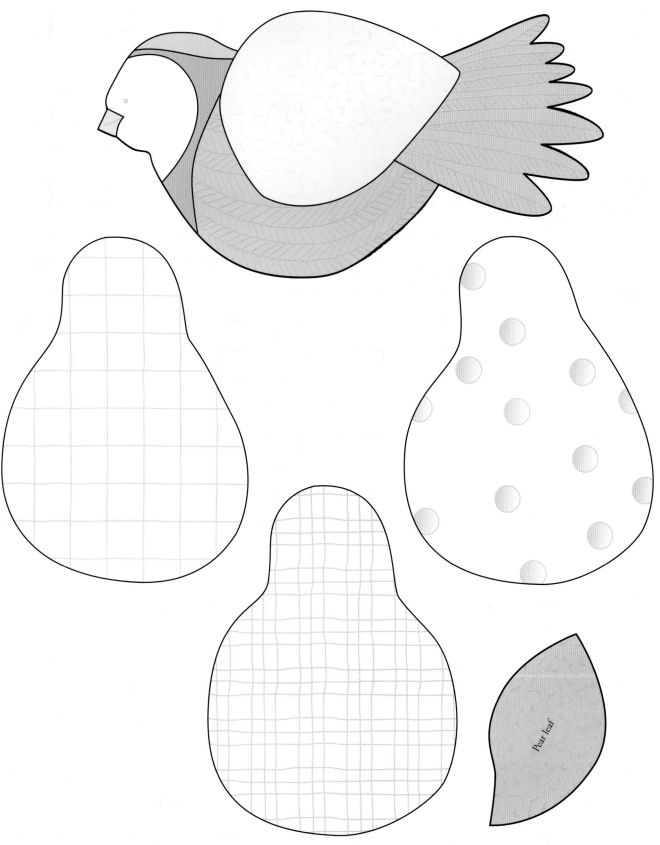

Pear leaf

PARTRIDGE AND PEAR TEMPLATES

12 DRUMMERS DRUMMING

*O*n the twelfth day of Christmas,
my true love sent to me,
Twelve Drummers Drumming ...

Celebrate the twelfth day with the same joy
as the very first ... and let the generous
spirit of The Twelve Days of Christmas
warm your heart the whole year through.

TWELFTH HOUR QUILT

It's not too late! You may be down to the "twelfth hour" in your busy Christmas preparations, but you can still create this wonderfully eye-catching quilt. With its elegant velvet borders, it's perfect for a special friend ... but you may just decide to keep it for yourself!

Finished Size: 54" x 68"

FABRIC REQUIREMENTS

Fabric A (*red #1*) - ¾ yard
Fabric B (*red #2*) - ¼ yard
Fabric C (*red #3*) - ⅛ yard
Fabric D (*green #1*) - ⅜ yard
Fabric E (*green #2*) - ⅓ yard
Fabric F (*green #3*) - ⅛ yard
Fabric G (*cream #1*) - ½ yard
Fabric H (*cream #2*) - ½ yard
Fabric I (*gold #1*) - ⅓ yard
Fabric J (*gold #2*) - ¼ yard
Fabric K (*black #1*) - ⅓ yard
Fabric L (*black #2*) - ⅓ yard
Inside Border (*dark green*)
  ½ yard

Accent Border (*gold #3*)
  ¼ yard
Outside Border (*black velvet*)
  2 yards*
Binding - ⅝ yard
Backing - 3⅓ yards
Batting - 60" x 74" piece
Fusible web

*If you prefer traditional cotton fabric for borders, substitute 1 yard black cotton print.

12 DRUMMERS DRUMMING

CUTTING THE STRIPS AND PIECES

Read first paragraph of Cutting the Strips and Pieces on page 14.

Fabric A (*red #1*)
Two 4½" x 42" strips, cut into
- Five 4½" x 8½" pieces
One 7½" x 40½" strip
Two 3" x 42" strips

Fabric B (*red #2*)
Two 3" x 42" strips

Fabric C (*red #3*)
One 2½" x 40½" strip

Fabric D (*green #1*)
Two 4½" x 42" strips, cut into
- Ten 4½" squares
One 2½" x 40½" strip

Fabric E (*green #2*)
One 5½" x 42" strip
One 2½" x 40½" strip

Fabric F (*green #3*)
One 2½" x 40½" strip

Fabric G (*cream #1*)
Two 4½" x 42" strips, cut into
- Ten 4½" squares
Two 3" x 42" strips

Fabric H (*cream #2*)
Three 2½" x 42" strips
Two 3" x 42" strips

Fabric I (*gold #1*)
One 2½" x 40½" strip
Set remainder aside for stars.

Fabric J (*gold #2*)
One 5½" x 42" strip

Fabric K (*black #1*)
Three 2½" x 42" strips
One 2½" x 40½" strip

Fabric L (*black #2*)
Two 4½" x 42" strips, cut into
- Five 4½" x 8½" pieces

Inside Border (*dark green*)
Two 2½" x 40½" strips
Three 2½" x42" strips

Accent Border (*gold #3*)
Six 1" x 42" strips

Outside Border (*black velvet*)
* Four 4½" x 72" strips
* *Velvet border strips are cut from fabric lengthwise to avoid visible piecing seams. If cutting from cotton fabric crosswise, cut six 4½" x 42" strips.*

Binding - Seven 2¾" x 42" strips

MAKING THE PIECED STRIPS

1. Referring to Quick-Corner Triangles on page 138, sew a 4½" Fabric D square to each 4½" x 8½" Fabric A piece. Press.

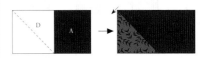

2. Sew remaining 4½" Fabric D squares to units from step 1.

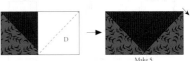

Make 5.

3. Sew units from step 2 together in one long row and add 2½" x 40½" Fabric I strip to bottom edge. Press.

4. Repeat steps 1-3 with 4½" Fabric G squares and 4½" x 8½" Fabric L pieces, adding 2½" x 40½" Fabric C strip to bottom edge and 2½" x 40½" Fabric D strip to top edge. Press.

5. Sew two 3" x 42" Fabric B strips to two 3" x 42" Fabric G strips, alternating the colors. Press. Cut four 8½"-wide segments from strip-pieced unit.

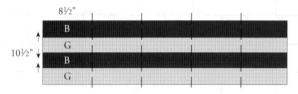

6. Sew segments from step 5 together to make one long row. Add 2½" x 40½" Fabric E strip to bottom edge.

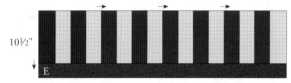

7. Repeat steps 5 and 6, using 3" x 42" Fabric A and H strips, but do not sew a strip across bottom edge.

8. Sew 5½" x 42" Fabric E strip to 5½" x 42" Fabric J strip. Press. Cut four 5½"-wide segments from strip-pieced unit.

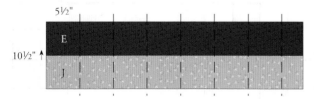

9. Sew segments from step 8 together to make one long strip. Sew 2½" x 40½" Fabric K strip to bottom edge.

10. Sew 2½" x 42" Fabric H strip between two 2½" x 42" Fabric K strips. Press. Cut into ten 2½" x 6½" segments.

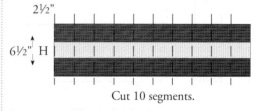

Cut 10 segments.

11. Sew 2½" x 42" Fabric K strip between two 2½" x 42" Fabric H strips. Press. Cut ten 2½" x 6½" segments. Press.

12. Sew segments from steps 10 and 11 to make a checkerboard strip. Sew 2½" x 40½" Fabric F strip to bottom edge. Press. Sew 7½" x 40½" Fabric A strip to bottom edge of strip F.

13. Referring to Quick-Fuse Appliqué on page 139, cut and fuse five stars from remaining Fabric I. Space stars evenly across strip. Zigzag stitch over raw edges.

ASSEMBLY

1. Referring to quilt layout on page 129, sew pieced strips together in correct order.

2. Sew 2½" x 40½" inside border strips to top and bottom edges of quilt top. Press seams toward borders. Cut one 2½" x 42" inside border strip in half and sew one piece to each of remaining 2½" x 42" inside border strip. From each long strip, cut one 2½" x 58½" strip. Sew to sides of quilt top. Press seams toward borders.

3. Cut two 1" x 42" accent border strips in half and sew one piece to each of four remaining 1" x 42" accent border strips. Sew accent borders to top and bottom edges of quilt top, trim excess border and press seams toward accent border. Sew remaining accent border strips to long edges of quilt top.

4. Measure quilt top width across center and cut two black velvet border strips to this measurement. Hand baste, then sew to top and bottom edges of quilt top. Finger press.

5. Measure quilt top length through center and cut two black velvet border strips to this measurement. Hand baste, then sew to long edges of quilt top. Finger press.

LAYERING AND FINISHING

1. Cut backing fabric crosswise into two equal pieces. Sew together to make one 60" x 84" piece. Trim to match size of batting piece.

2. Arrange and baste backing, batting, and quilt top together, referring to Layering the Quilt on page 138.

3. Machine or hand quilt as desired.

4. Cut two binding strips in half and sew halves to each of remaining four binding strips. Bind quilt, referring to Binding the Quilt on page 139.

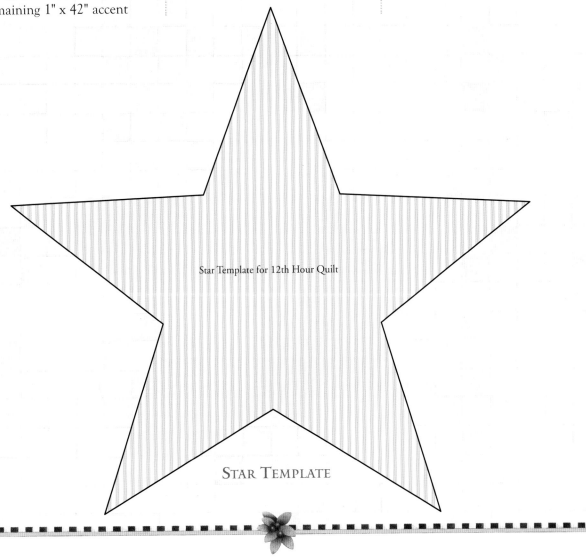

Star Template for 12th Hour Quilt

STAR TEMPLATE

WOOL ORNAMENTS

The partridge, the French hen, the Lord-a-Leaping … and all the rest. Inspired by your favorite and fanciful characters from the Twelve Days of Christmas, these folk-art style wool ornaments are sure to become cherished family treasures.

MATERIALS NEEDED

Felted wool - assorted scraps in several solid colors plus plaids and herringbone designs

Paper-backed fusible web

Embroidery floss in assorted colors

Scrap of narrow ribbon *(for wreath)*

Small beads

Beaded gold rings *(for wreath)* - Five

Assorted small beads for embellishments

Decorative cord for loops

GENERAL DIRECTIONS FOR ORNAMENTS

1. Use the patterns on pages 133-137 to make templates for each ornament. In all cases, piece #1 is the entire outside outline of the layered pieces. For most ornaments, you will need to cut two of each piece #1. (Exceptions are the pipe, dancing shoes, and milk bucket.) Refer to cutting directions with each ornament pattern.

2. Apply paper-backed fusible web to each chosen fabric scrap.

3. Trace and cut the required pieces for each ornament.

4. Fuse pieces to piece #1 in numerical order.

5. Blanket stitch over all edges with 3 strands of embroidery floss in a contrasting color.

6. Referring to Embroidery Stitch Guide on page 138 and individual ornament patterns, add embroidered details. Use French knots for eyes and satin stitch for birds' beaks.

7. Embellish with beads as desired.

8. Cut 4½" length of cord for a hanging loop for each ornament. Knot each end. Tack knots to back of ornament with a few hand stitches.

Sew knots to back of ornament

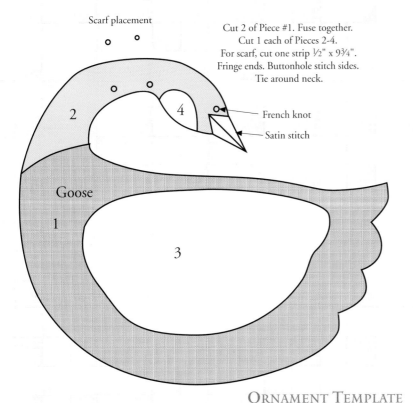

Scarf placement

Cut 2 of Piece #1. Fuse together.
Cut 1 each of Pieces 2-4.
For scarf, cut one strip ½" x 9¾".
Fringe ends. Buttonhole stitch sides.
Tie around neck.

French knot

Satin stitch

Goose

2

4

1

3

ORNAMENT TEMPLATE

Wreath pattern

Cut 2.
Fuse together.
Embelish with
ribbon, buttons
and stitching.

4

1

2

Embroider and
bead stripes.

3

Dancing shoes

Cut 1 of outline.
Cut 1 each of Pieces 2, 3 and 4.
Fuse together.

ORNAMENT TEMPLATES

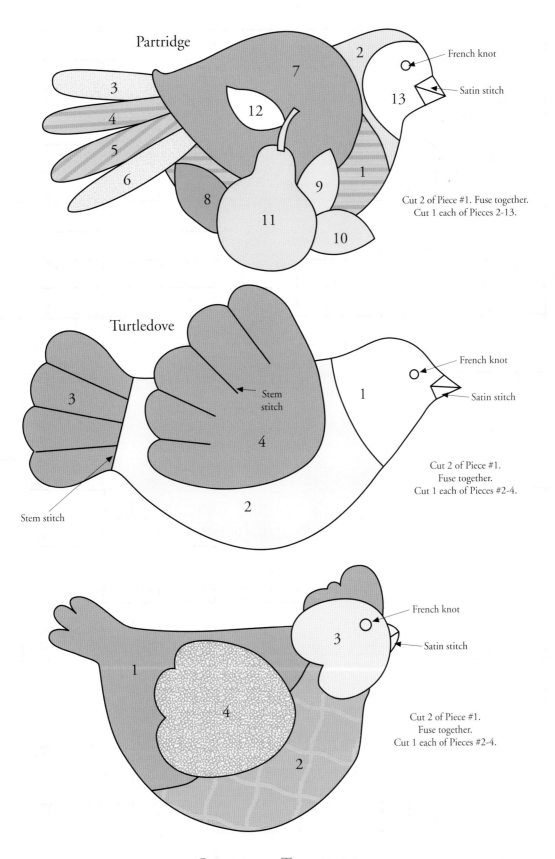

Partridge

French knot

Satin stitch

Cut 2 of Piece #1. Fuse together.
Cut 1 each of Pieces 2-13.

Turtledove

French knot

Satin stitch

Stem stitch

Stem stitch

Cut 2 of Piece #1.
Fuse together.
Cut 1 each of Pieces #2-4.

French knot

Satin stitch

Cut 2 of Piece #1.
Fuse together.
Cut 1 each of Pieces #2-4.

ORNAMENT TEMPLATES

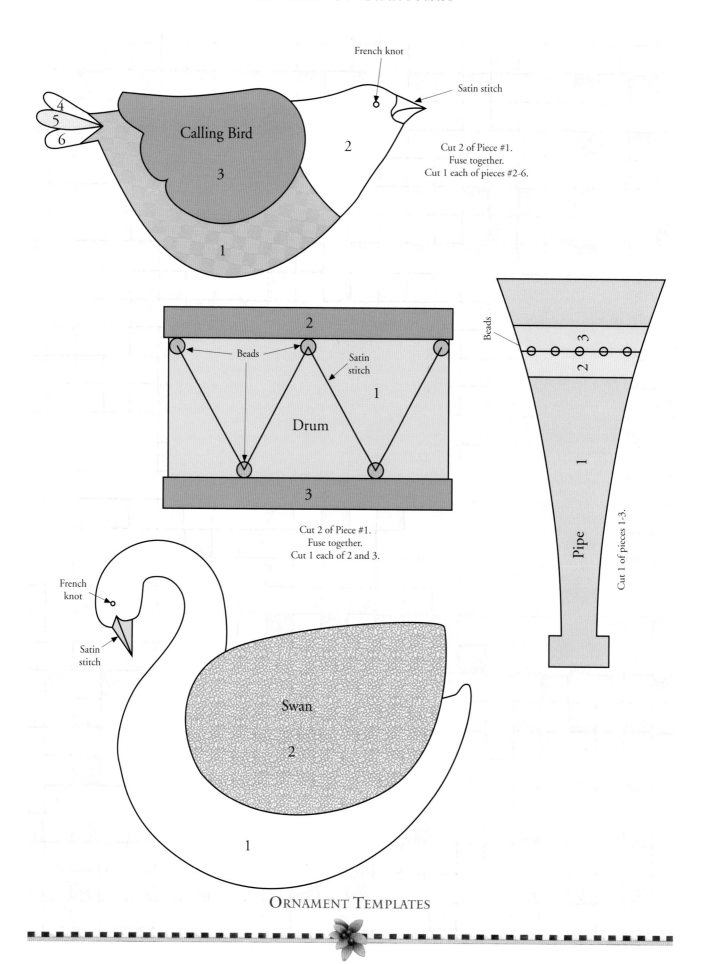

French knot

Satin stitch

Calling Bird

4
5
6

3

2

1

Cut 2 of Piece #1.
Fuse together.
Cut 1 each of pieces #2-6.

Beads

2

Satin
stitch

1

Drum

3

Cut 2 of Piece #1.
Fuse together.
Cut 1 each of 2 and 3.

Beads

2 3

2

1

Pipe

Cut 1 of pieces 1-3.

French
knot

Satin
stitch

Swan

2

1

ORNAMENT TEMPLATES

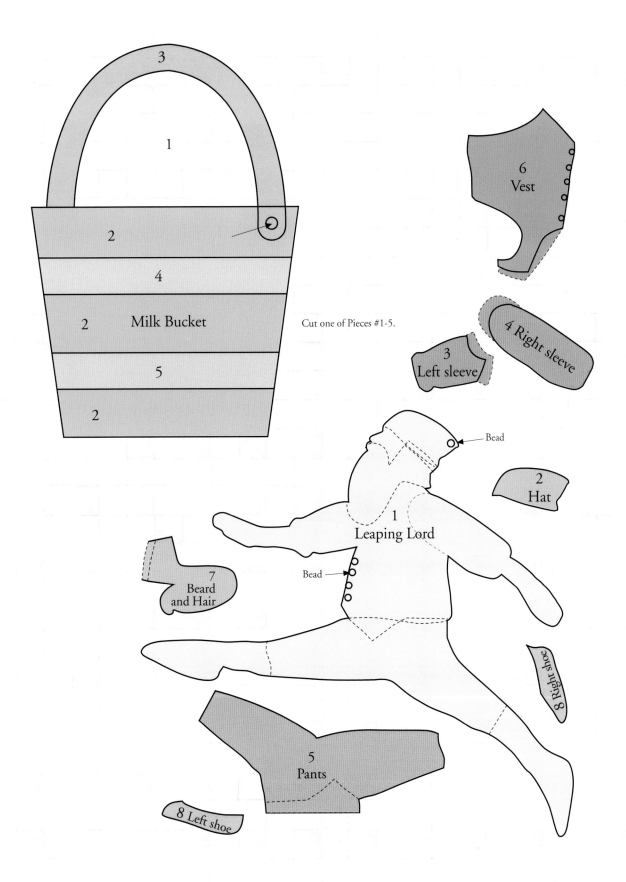

3

1

2

4

2   Milk Bucket

5

2

Cut one of Pieces #1-5.

6
Vest

4 Right sleeve

3
Left sleeve

Bead

2
Hat

1
Leaping Lord

7
Beard
and Hair

Bead

8 Right shoe

5
Pants

8 Left shoe

ORNAMENT TEMPLATES

GENERAL DIRECTIONS

HAND APPLIQUÉ

Hand appliqué is easy when you start out with the right supplies. Cotton machine embroidery thread is easy to work with. Pick a color that matches the appliqué fabric as closely as possible. Use a long, thin needle like a sharp for stitching, and slender appliqué or silk pins for holding shapes in place.

1. Make a plastic template for every shape in the appliqué design. Use a dotted line to show where pieces overlap.
2. Place template on right side of appliqué fabric. Trace around template.
3. Cut out shapes ¼" beyond traced line.

4. Position shapes on background fabric. For pieces that overlap, follow numbers on patterns. Pieces with lower numbers go underneath; pieces with higher numbers are layered on top. Pin shapes in place.
5. Stitch shapes in order following pattern numbers. Where shapes overlap, do not turn under and stitch edges of bottom pieces. Turn and stitch the edges of the piece on top.

6. Use the traced line as your turn-under guide. Entering from the wrong side of the appliqué shape, bring the needle up on the traced line. Using the tip of the needle, turn under the fabric along the traced line. Using a blind stitch, stitch along the folded edge to join the appliqué shape to the background fabric. Turn under and stitch only about ¼" at a time.
7. Clip curves and V-shapes to help the fabric turn under smoothly. Clip to within a couple threads of the traced line. When you're done stitching the entire block, place it face down on top of a thick towel and press.

QUICK CORNER TRIANGLES

Quick corner triangles are formed by simply sewing fabric squares to other squares and rectangles. The directions and diagrams with each project show you what size pieces to use and where to place square on corresponding piece. See fabric key with each project for fabric identification. Follow steps 1-3 below to make corner triangle units.

1. With pencil and ruler, draw diagonal line on wrong side of fabric square that will form the triangle. See Diagram A. This will be your sewing line.

   A.
   sewing line

   B.
   trim ¼" away from sewing line

   C.
   finished corner triangle unit

2. With right sides together, place square on corresponding piece. Matching raw edges, pin in place and sew ON drawn line.
3. Press seam in direction of arrow as shown in step-by-step project diagram. Trim off excess fabric leaving ¼" seam allowance as shown in Diagram B. Measure completed corner triangle unit to ensure greatest accuracy.

EMBROIDERY STITCH GUIDE

Blanket Stitch   Chain Stitch
French Knot   Lazy Daisy Stitch
Satin Stitch   Running Stitch
Stem Stitch   Cross Stitch

LAYERING THE QUILT

1. Cut backing and batting 3" to 6" larger than quilt top.
2. Lay pressed backing on bottom (right side down), batting in middle, and pressed quilt top on top. Make sure everything is centered and that backing and batting are flat. Backing and batting will extend beyond quilt top.
3. Begin basting in center and work toward outer edges. Baste vertically and horizontally, forming a 3" to 4" grid. Baste or pin completely around edge of quilt top. Trim batting and backing to ¼" from raw edge of quilt top.

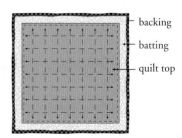

backing
batting
quilt top

BINDING THE QUILT

1. Fold and press binding strips in half lengthwise with wrong sides together.
2. With raw edges even, lay binding strips on top and bottom edges of quilt top. Sew through all layers, ¼" from quilt edge. Press binding away from quilt top. Trim excess length of binding.
3. Sew remaining two binding strips to quilt sides. Press and trim excess length.
4. Folding top and bottom first, fold binding around to back. Press and pin in position. Hand stitch binding in place.

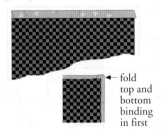

← fold top and bottom binding in first

QUICK-FUSE APPLIQUÉ

Quick-fuse appliqué is a method of adhering appliquè pieces to a background with fusible web. For quick and easy results, simply quick-fuse appliqué pieces in place. Use non-sewable, heavyweight fusible web such as HeatnBond Ultrahold. For some projects, finishing edges of appliqué pieces with a hand or machine stitch may be desired. Use sewable, lightweight fusible web, such as HeatnBond Lite, for these projects. Laundering is not recommended unless edges are finished.

1. With paper side up, lay fusible web over appliqué design. Leaving ½" space between pieces, trace all elements of design. Cut around traced pieces, approximately ¼" outside traced line. See Diagram A.
2. With paper side up, position and iron fusible web to wrong side of selected fabrics. Follow manufacturer's directions for iron temperature and fusing time. Cut out each piece on traced line. See Diagram B.

A. fusible web

B. fabric-wrong side

3. Remove paper backing from pieces. A thin film will remain on wrong side. Position and fuse all pieces of one appliquè design at a time onto background, referring to color photos for placement.

PAINTING TECHNIQUES

Transforming readymade pots and other decorative accessories with paint is fun and easy. To get you started painting the projects in this book, here are some basic instructions. Read these before you begin any painting project.

PAINTING ON METAL

1. Wipe down galvanized objects with vinegar before painting. This is a must! Spray with flat metal primer.
2. Apply base coat with acrylic paint. Most surfaces require two coats. Use inexpensive foam brushes.
3. Add surface textures such as sponging, spattering, or crackling.

To sponge, apply contrasting color with a textured sponge.
To spatter, apply contrasting color by running your thumb over a paint-filled toothbrush. Always test this on paper first.
To crackle, purchase a commercial medium and follow manufacturer's instructions.

4. Add painted details as shown in each project photo.

When adding checks and stripes, apply the lightest color first. Paint stripes or checks over the lighter base coat. Draw pattern with a ruler and soft-lead pencil to keep lines straight. Use *Scotch® Brand™* Magic tape to mask areas and create an edge to paint against for really straight lines. Be sure other painted areas are thoroughly dry before pressing tape into place.

5. Spray or brush on a coat of matte-finish varnish.
6. For an aged look, apply antiquing medium. Many products are available in both oil-base and latex formulas. Follow manufacturer's instructions for best results.
7. Add a final coat of varnish in either matte, satin, or gloss finish.

PAINTING TERRA COTTA

1. Prime pot inside and out with gesso and allow to dry thoroughly.
2. Proceed with steps 2-10 above.
3. Be sure to place a plastic liner inside pot before adding a live plant.

Ordering Information
Porcelain Buttons: The Porcelain Rose
P.O. Box 7545
Long Beach, CA 90807
(562) 424-9728

DISCOVER MORE FROM DEBBIE MUMM

Here's a sampling of the many quilting and home décor books by Debbie Mumm®.
These books and specially designed patterns are available at your local quilt shop,
by calling (888) 819-2923, or by shopping online at *www.debbiemumm.com*.

Debbie Mumm's®
Floral Inspirations
80-page, soft cover

Debbie Mumm's®
Birdhouses for Every Season
112-page, soft cover

Debbie Mumm's®
Country Settings
112-page, soft cover

Debbie Mumm®
Celebrates
The Holidays at Home
80-page, soft cover

Debbie Mumm® Quilts
Santa's Scrapbook
112-page, soft cover

Noah's Noel
40-page, soft cover

Debbie Mumm® Salutes
America the Beautiful
32-page, soft cover

Debbie Mumm's®
Sweet Baby Dreams
24-page, soft cover

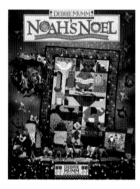

Angel Wings &
Growing Things
40-page, soft cover

Book titles limited to stock on hand.
Products may be discontinued at any time by Debbie Mumm, Inc.

Debbie Mumm, Inc.
1116 E. Westview Court
Spokane, WA 99218-1384

www.debbiemumm.com

Toll Free (888) 819-2923
(509) 466-3572
Fax (509) 466-6919

CREDITS

Designed by Debbie Mumm®
Special thanks to my creative teams:

EDITORIAL/PROJECT DESIGN
Mya Brooks: Production Director
Carolyn Lowe: Quilt and
Craft Designer
Susan Nelsen: Quilt and
Craft Designer
Jean Van Bockel: Quilt and
Craft Designer
Jackie Saling: Craft Designer
Candy Huddleston: Seamstress
Nona King: Machine Quilter
Wanda Jeffries: Machine Quilter
Nancy Kirkland: Quilter
Anna Marie Harlow: Menu

GRAPHICS TEAM
Tom Harlow: Production Manager
Sherry Hassel: Senior Graphic Designer
Nancy Hanlon: Graphic Designer
Heather Hughes: Graphic Designer

ART TEAM
Lou McKee, Senior Artist
Kathy Arbuckle
Sandy Ayars
Heather Butler
Gil-Jin Foster
Kathy Riedinger

BOOK DESIGN & PRODUCTION

Sea-Hill Press, Inc.
Lynnwood, Washington
Greg Sharp: President
Barbara Weiland: Writer
Laura M. Reinstatler: Editor
Pamela Mostek: Copy Editor
Barbara Schmitt: Art Director
Heather Bauerle: Graphic Asst.
Brian Metz: Illustrator
Melanie Blair: Photography
Sinclaire Fornasir: Photo Stylist
Christy Nordstrom: Food Stylist

©2000 Debbie Mumm, Inc.
Revised 3/2002

Printed in China